ProActive
Sales Management

How to Lead, Motivate, and Stay Ahead of the Game

SECOND EDITION

William "Skip" Miller

American Management Association

New York • Atlanta • Brussels • Chicago • Mexico City • San Francisco
Shanghai • Tokyo • Toronto • Washington, D. C.

This publication is designed to provide accurate and authoritative information in regard to the subject matter covered. It is sold with the understanding that the publisher is not engaged in rendering legal, accounting, or other professional service. If legal advice or other expert assistance is required, the services of a competent professional person should be sought.

Library of Congress Cataloging-in-Publication Data

Miller, William
    ProActive sales management : how to lead, motivate, and stay ahead of the game / William "Skip" Miller.—2nd ed.
        p.   cm.
    Includes bibliographical references and index.
    ISBN 978-0-8144-1456-9
    ISBN-10: 0-8144-1456-7
    1. Sales management.   I. Title.

    HF5438.4.M543   2009
    658.8'1—dc22

                                                    2009002852

Printing number

10   9   8   7   6   5   4   3

Contents

Contents

Acknowledgments

This is for all the Sales Managers who get it. The ones who get having faith, trust, and confidence. To the managers who put in the extra effort and let the salespeople thrive, as opposed to putting them through the inquisition every week. Especially the ones who tell their salespeople to go ahead and try, even though they have never tried it, and letting go just seems so hard.

Nowhere in the organization is performance so visible. You are doing a great job by getting things done through others.

To my business friends and clients; this could never happen without you. Thank you very, very, much.

To the thousands of salespeople . . . we are trying to make them smarter. Be patient please.

As always, to my family. You are the reason. To Susan, you are my purpose.

Preface to the Second Edition

"If you don't know how you are going to do one month into the quarter, head for Las Vegas, You have better odds of making money there than you do with your sales forecast."

—Skip Miller

Sales managers are still doing the wrong thing, same as they were 10 years ago. Oh, some managers are very successful: Year after year, they achieve their revenue goals, lead successful teams, and enjoy successful careers. They are working late, working weekends, traveling up to three weeks a month, and they tell themselves they are doing the job. They are not. The job is doing it to them.

They are reactive and cannot see any way out. So they work like dogs. They end up looking dog-tired because of it. There has got to be a better way, and of course there is. A simpler way to be more effective than ever before. A ProActive way.

ProActive Sales Management clearly identifies what qualities are needed for the successful sales manager. It provides a step-by-step method you can use to change the way you manage—and begin to manage ProActively. By reading and implementing the tactics and processes in *ProActive Sales Management*, you will be able to:

- Accomplish more in less time.
- Be ProActive and live in the future.

- Motivate salespeople to highly motivate themselves.
- Focus on A players and turn them into A+ players.
- Establish a ProActive culture and let the people manage themselves.
- Increase the effectiveness of your day-to-day management job.
- Decrease the time you spend on noneffective tasks and reports.
- Predict and forecast the future with greater accuracy.
- Increase your ability to interview and hire correctly.
- Successfully implement a set of metrics that you can use in a ProActive and behavior-predicting manner.
- Effectively use coaching and counseling techniques.
- Manage to metrics that make sense.

Why There Is a Burning Need for Managers to Change

Stephen Covey states, "I expand my personal freedom and influence through being proactive." He is right, and this kind of thinking needs to be addressed within the organization that is required to be forward thinking, freedom loving, and ProActive: the customer-centric sales organization.

Sales managers, however, never receive the training they need or require to do their job ProActively. Successful people who are soon to be effective sales managers need to know what is expected of them *before* they enter the world of sales management.

Current sales management needs to go "back to the basics" and focus on getting things done through others rather than using the reactive characteristics and behaviors that got them promoted into management, such as being a super salesperson. It is the *reactive* nature of their sales job that permeates the sales management ranks today, and that reactive culture has become the norm.

These days, speed is the name of the game. It's no longer how many sales calls, but how many customer or prospect touches. Not how long does a sale take, but how long are you spending at each step. ProActive tools are no longer just nice to have. ProActive selling is *the* way to sell in an increasing competitive, cost-efficient manner.

Is being reactive the nature of the sales management beast? Are most sales managers reactive? How much time do you spend being reactive on a day-to-day basis? How reactive are you? Let's take a simple test to find out. Please circle the response that applies to you.

QUIZ: How Reactive Are You?

1. How many voice mails, e-mails, or text messages do you get a day?

   a) Less than 5
   b) Between 5 and 10
   c) Between 10 and 15
   d) Between 15 and 25
   e) More than 25

2. Of the last 10 sales situations you were involved in as a manager, how many times did you have to interject a vital piece of information or even "take over the call"?

   a) None
   b) 1 to 3
   c) 4 to 6
   d) 7 to 8
   e) All of them, are you kidding, that's what I am there for!

3. Do you have:

   a) One phone and one e-mail address
   b) One phone, one e-mail address, and a cell phone
   c) One phone, one e-mail address, two cell phones, and a pager
   d) Office phone, cell phone, pager, two cell phones, e-mail address (office), e-mail (home), fax machine, laptop, and a palmtop or PDA or Blackberry
   e) Multiple of any items of d above

4. If you ranked your sales team members on an A, B, or C scale (with A being your top performers), which of the following patterns most closely resembles the proportion of time you spend with each group?

   a) 80 percent on As, 10 percent on Bs, 10 percent on Cs
   b) 60 percent on As, 30 percent on Bs, 10 percent on Cs
   c) 40 percent on As, 30 percent on Bs, 30 percent on Cs
   d) 30 percent on As, 20 percent on Bs, 50 percent on Cs
   e) 10 percent on As, 20 percent on Bs, 70 percent on Cs

5. What percentage of your office time per week do you spend planning one to three months or three to six months out?

   a) 25 to 30 percent
   b) 20 percent
   c) 10 percent
   d) 5 percent
   e) Have to make the number *today!* No time for the future.

5. What percentage of the day do you spend with your A+ salespeople?

   a) 25 to 30 percent
   b) 20 percent
   c) 10 percent
   d) 5 percent
   e) Let them do what they do the best. I've got a ton of other problems.

If you answered d or e to any or all of the items, you need to be more ProActive, and this book is required reading for you.

Quit having useless meetings. Give up focusing internally on past revenue numbers. Stop having those quarterly reviews that focus on what happened the *last* three months. Quit guessing on what you need to hire and fill those open head counts within 30 days. Start being one step ahead of the game.

Three things before we begin.

- We use the terms "sales manager" and "sales management" interchangeably throughout the book. When we say sales manager or sales management, we mean all management levels, from first-line sales manager to executive sales management.

- We spell the words "proactive" and "proactively" as *Pro-Active* and *ProActively* to remind you that there is a new way to manage: a ProActive way; a better and more effective way. The tools in this book are going to change the way you manage. The way you look at your job. The way you think. It will put you one step ahead.

- This is the second revision to *ProActive Sales Management*, and you will find very few changes from the original book. But we made additions where they were needed to adapt to the current times. And we added some new ideas. If you already own the original, these additions should make rereading this book worthwhile.

Chapter 1

ProActive Sales Manager—Defining the New Breed of Sales Manager

ProActive Sales Manager. What a title. Who wouldn't want to be a ProActive manager? Who wouldn't want to be one step ahead? One leg up on everyone else. Always prepared for the crisis situation. Having the right answers for the right questions in the quarterly management sales review. Knowing where to spend your time and resources wisely—ProActively.

By definition, "ProActive" means ahead of the game, someone who always thinks before she acts, and someone who is one or two moves ahead of the competition. Some people dislike the word "ProActive," probably because they are so *re*active they just reject the notion that anyone can be any different. But ProActive sales managers do exist. They are few in number, but they can be found.

How can you become one of the ProActive elite? What does it take? We have been observing and working with sales management on this exact topic for years. Highly competent sales managers have the ability to *spend their limited resources on the situation that needs to be addressed.* How do they do it? It's not magic. They do it by being ProActive.

You are about to embark on a journey through the day-to-day tasks of sales management. We focus on the tactical aspects of the sales manager's roles and responsibilities, such as what questions to ask during an interview, how to conduct a sales meeting, how to motivate, and what specific metrics you should measure to. However, the overlying *strategic* theme is about being ProActive.

Being ProActive doesn't mean waking up in the morning and deciding, "Hey, today I am going to be ProActive and get ahead of all my tasks for the day." It is not the latest overused buzzword. "I'm ProActive. Are you ProActive?" Short-term, buzzword approaches to being ProActive may work on any given day, but it requires a tremendous amount of energy, and it might not be possible to sustain.

Everyone has "power days," when they feel they have a tremendous amount of energy and can take on the world. These short bursts of ProActivity last only a few hours. Why? The rest of the world forgot you were trying to be ProActive and has now conspired to change your agenda, or at least reverse your direction. There are even canned phrases for this *reversal effect*, which is illustrated by the following quotes:

- "I was doing so well; then my boss came in with his agenda and shot the rest of my day."
- "The day started out really strong; then the fires came. Why is it I spend better than half my day putting out these fires? And they are not even my fires!"
- "How did this happen? All of a sudden, I had the monkey on my back, and I was being assigned to tasks that should have been on other people's agendas. Too many monkeys and now I am working everyone else's to-do list but my own!"

These are actual quotes taken from sales management training seminars. We all have good intentions and want to be ProActive. Being ProActive is not a task, but a strategy. It allows you to complete the day-to-day tasks under the umbrella of ProActivity. It is a way for you to make decisions that affect the future, not the past, and to work to your own agenda, not someone else's. Work to your priorities, not to the priority *du jour*. ProActive sales managers are ProActive on the overall strategy, as well as the day-to-day tactical decisions. It is a way of effectively managing and invoking a much-requested discipline on themselves. It ends up becoming part of their culture.

How do you begin on this journey that will allow you to do more in less time and be effective beyond belief? You begin by finding out what the sales manager's actual role and responsibility is.

What Is the Actual Role of the Sales Manager?

Sales leadership. That's it. By any other name, this is what companies and employees want in a sales manager. For an effective sales manager, leadership is the key ingredient. How do you acquire leadership? What makes sales managers effective leaders? Let's solve the Leadership Puzzle (see Figure 1-1).

A quick story. Bob remembers when he first became a sales manager—both a wonderful and scary proposition. He had been a very competent salesperson. "Quite arrogant, some may say. I was a good salesperson with a high degree of ego thrown into the mix."

Figure I-I. Leadership Puzzle.

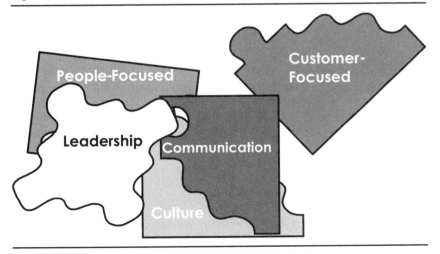

Bob's first manager at the time, Kevin, was a very effective sales director, one of the best. Well, when a first-line sales management position opened up, Kevin offered it to him, but a bit reluctantly. "Kevin was not sure about my ability to transition from selling to managing, whatever that meant," he confided. After assuring Kevin in his most straightforward and brash manner (he thought it was confidence) that he could do the job, they had a great discussion. Finally, Kevin asked what reservations he had about the job. Bob still remembers looking Kevin straight in the eyes and saying, "I know I can do the job. But there is one thing that escapes me. How do you get salespeople to respect you? How do you lead them?"

Kevin's response was, "You just took a towel, put it in between my ears, and cleaned out all the reservations I had about you being a successful manager. Let's get started."

Respect and leadership. How do you ProActively acquire these traits? For an answer, let's look at five key questions in the leadership puzzle.

1. What makes a successful salesperson?
2. What makes a successful sales manager?
3. What are the similarities between the two?
4. What tasks does the sales manager perform on a day-to-day basis?
5. What are the expectations placed on the sales manager?

Figure 1-2 shows some typical responses to these questions, taken from actual responses given at our sales management courses. So what do these questions tell us? What is to be gained from this exercise? Let's take it one question at a time.

What Makes a Successful Salesperson?

First, what are the characteristics of a good salesperson? Aggressive, personable, product smart, never quits, empathetic, good listener, and so on. The list in Figure 1-2 is not complete by any means, but it does reveal an overall trend: a strong *customer focus*. The successful salesperson has been trained and has learned to focus his skills and attention on the customer. This

Figure 1-2. Answers to leadership puzzle questions.

Successful Salesperson

- Is aggressive.
- Is a winner.
- Is personable.
- Can prioritize.
- Knows when to call for help.
- Is product smart.
- Is a good listener.

- Takes direction well.
- Is empathetic.
- Works the system.
- Is a team player.
- Is a good presenter.
- Treats the customer as #1.
- Never quits.

- Has time management skills.
- Closes the deal.
- Is money motivated.
- Has a good image/appearance.

Successful Sales Manager

- Is a good listener.
- Gets things done through others.
- Hires effectively.
- Is company-focused.
- Has no knee jerks.

- Has coaching skills.
- Is a motivator.
- Is good at corrective action.
- Is a trainer.
- Is a good communicator.

- Has time management skills.
- Has counseling skills.
- Is a mentor.
- Keeps perspective.
- Is well informed.

Similarities

- Is a good listener.
- Is a team player.
- Has same goals.

- Is well informed.
- Can prioritize.
- Is a problem solver.

- Has time management skills.
- Is empathetic.
- Is respectful.

Daily Tasks

- Reports.
- Motivates.
- Puts out fires.
- Attends staff meetings.
- Performs territory reviews.
- Goes on coaching calls.

- Communicates.
- Thinks about the future.
- Recruits candidates.
- Handles customer complaints.
- Inspires.

- Forecasts.
- Prioritizes resources.
- Performs sales reviews.
- Performs product reviews.

Expectations

- Makes the numbers.
- Manages the boss.
- Gives market input.
- Is fair.
- Has vision.
- Hires good people.

- Has high ethics.
- Is financially focused.
- Thinks of all departments.
- Is a good listener.
- Has good communication skills.

- Promotes good people.
- Has a company-first mentality.
- Has good judgment.
- Is a liaison—management/sales team.

overriding trait is necessary for salespeople to be successful. They focus on the customer.

How do salespeople get to this point? When does a salesperson stop working for the company and start working for the customer? Let's take a look at a typical scenario.

When Jill, a rookie salesperson, is just starting out, the company does some limited amount of training: some sales training, some product training, and some presentation skills training. All training is focused on helping her deal with the customer. Then, the company points her to the front door and tells her to go sell. Go get orders.

She heads for the door, goes out, and makes a few calls: "Hi, I'm Jill, and I would like a few minutes of your time."

BAM, she gets the proverbial door slammed in her face. Undaunted, she tries again: "Hi, I'm Jill and . . ."

BAM, it happens again. Well, after a few more BAMs, the rookie gets a little street smart and figures out how to at least get in the door (another learned *customer-focused* selling skill).

So, after a rough start, she is in the door and progressing through a sale. She finally gets a live one and a chance to actually close a deal. She now takes the offer back to the boss. Of course, this deal is a little bit unusual, with a little too much discount, tight shipping terms, and very liberal payment terms. But hey, it's a deal.

Of course the boss does not look too favorably on this deal. He rejects it and tells Jill, "You have to do better."

Jill tells her boss, "The customer is seriously entertaining a competitive offer. We have to accept this deal, or we will lose the order."

The transformation has taken place. It never fails. The salesperson is looking at the order and knows she can close it. If only her company were a little more flexible; a little more reasonable. The company is not in touch with the competitive landscape and needs to be a bit more understanding. The company is standing in the way of this order . . . my order! Transformation complete. The salesperson, who just moments before was a company person, someone who worked for the company, was trained by the company, and gets paid by the company, now works for the customer. This *customer focus* is illustrated by the following quotes:

"I work for the customer."

"I am the voice of the customer."

"We need to be a customer-focused company."

"If we did a better job of listening to the customers . . ."

"You pay me to get orders! The customer pays our bills."

So the stories go. The salesperson, knowing she needs to bring deals in to be employed and make a living, now finds it easier to side with the customer, and she continues to develop skills and traits to sharpen her customer-focused skill sets. To do this, she must become independent of the company. She now believes she is the voice of the customer, and if "the company" does not back her, then "the company" is nonresponsive. We train these salespeople to think independently, act independently, report independently, work independently, and sell independently. Is it any surprise they are company independent? They are now *customer-focused*. They have been trained, encouraged, and motivated to be this way.

When a deal is going down, it is much easier to side with the customer. After all, it is the customer who is paying the bills, and the company should be grateful for the orders that are coming in. Good, marginal, or whatever, an order is an order and the salesperson did the best she could to get the best deal. (Salespeople have great rationalization capabilities on what constitutes a good order.) So the company should take the deal.

Jill's experience is a bit exaggerated, but not too far from the truth. Good salespeople have developed these *customer-focused* skills into an art form and are very good at being the voice of the customer. The voice of the marketplace. The voice of the street. *Customer-focused*.

What Makes a Successful Sales Manager?

What makes a great manager? What separates the top managers from the mediocre ones? The ones who win time and time again—how do they do it? Again, the list in Figure 1-2 is not complete, but what you will find is that successful sales managers demonstrate strong people skills. Getting things done through others. They are *people-focused*. These skills differ from the skills you value in a salesperson.

Motivation, coaching, counseling, and mentoring are *people-focused* skills and traits that good sales managers need to get things done through others. However, these traits do not come from being a good salesperson.

Salespeople are customer-focused. Sales managers are people-focused. These skills are as different as night and day.

Successful salespeople *love* being the individual contributor. They love the independence, which to a large degree is what made them successful. But these customer-focused traits will not lead to success as a sales manager. Why? Sales managers need to work with and through people. They cannot act so independently.

It is no secret that some successful salespeople are not good at being sales managers. The reason is obvious. It is not what they were trained to do. They were trained to manage customers, not people. By the way, it may not be what they *want* to do either. Given the choice and the knowledge of what the two positions actually are, salespeople need to understand what the management job entails *before* they sign up, are recruited, or get commandeered.

In the "Newly Appointed Sales Manager" class that I have facilitated for the American Management Association for many years now, many of the new sales managers are still trying to "outsell" their current sales team members. "Do it my way," "I'll show you how to do it," or "This was how I was successful" are still prevalent attitudes among the newly appointed— and even some of the more experienced—sales managers.

The differences between customer-focused and people-focused skills are similar to the differences between being in school and being in the working world, or between being single and being married.

Do you remember all the skills you learned in order to get through school? How to cram? How to take tests? How to understand what the professor was looking for? How to sign up for the right class?

It's different in the working world, isn't it? No tests, no professors, no signing up for the easy class to get a good grade.

Do you remember when you were single? Maybe you still are. The skill sets you need when you are single are very different from those you need when you are married. When a recently married friend of mine had had a night out with "the boys" a few weeks after his honeymoon, he came home and announced to his wife that he was relieved because he still "had it." He explained that a few women had seemed interested enough in him to offer him their phone numbers. Of course he had no intention of calling these women, but it felt good to know that they had noticed him. Well, his wife did not share his relief. In fact, he discovered a new skill set, called "don't do it again."

- School/Working World Skill Sets
- Single/Married Skill Sets
- Salesperson/Sales Manager Skill Sets

These are all different ends of the skill spectrum. Sales managers need to be *people-focused*. They need to have the ability to get things done through others.

What Are the Similarities Between the Two Skills?

If we review the basic list shown in Figure 1-2, we will find that most of the similarities between the two jobs are in the people-centric skills, such as listening, being a team player, communicating, and being empathetic. If this is true, and if people-centered skills are crucial to the success of the organization, then what of the sales manager's #1 job? Where is his focus?

It must be centered on people skills, on getting things done through others. It must be ProActive in nature and allow for people to ProActively measure themselves against a standard. When all is said and done, the sales manager must put a stake in the ground and create an environment where people know what is important and what the rules are, and where salespeople are allowed to measure themselves to a standard. It is then the sales manager's #1 job to create this standard by *creating a culture*.

Now what the heck does this mean? Create a culture? Pro-Actively? This is the #1 job of a sales manager? What about revenue? What about hiring the right people? What about expense management? Creating a culture? Is this a bit theoretical? A bit Utopian, even?

Yes, *create a culture*. Be a *culture creator*. This is the sales manager's most important job. Why do we say this? Is creating a culture more important than meeting revenue goals, hiring smart people, or going on coaching sales calls? Yes, because while these are important tasks that consume much of your time each day, your primary goal as a sales manager is to get everyone in the organization working together—as one. Organizations that focus on certain objectives and goals have a great deal of leverage. The goals and objectives must be established and communicated.

Why is it winning teams always find a way to win, and losing teams always find a way to lose? Before their most recent change of ownership and management, baseball's Cleveland Indians had not finished higher than fourth place since 1954. They last won the World Series in 1948. When new management came in, they ushered in a new culture—a winning culture. In recent years the Indians have played in two World Series and have remained competitive in their division—after more than 40 years of losing baseball! Enter new management and—presto—they have a winning season almost every year. Go figure.

How did this happen? Certainly, there were many factors, but when asked, the new owners said it was the goal of their organization, including "every player and non-player, to establish a culture of winning and establish a winning tradition."

Be a ProActive *culture-creator*. This is your #1 job. It has the largest impact on the organization and all the tasks that lead up to winning. How do you do this? What needs to be done? Stay tuned and we will get to the details in Chapter 2.

What Tasks Does the Sales Manager Perform on a Day-to-Day Basis?

We now move to the sales manager's daily tasks, such as reporting, motivating, inspiring, forecasting, and performing sales reviews. What do these daily tasks have in common? Simple. They require you to become a *Master Communicator*. With good communication, both up and down the line, you become effective. This includes both formal and informal communication channels. Studies show that successful managers are ones who can effectively communicate their goals and objectives to all concerned. If the culture (job #1) is to be effective, you must communicate your business goals and objectives. You must communicate your culture and must become a *Master Communicator*.

It is not enough to know what to do. You have to know what to do, plus you have to do it. An effective sales manager needs the help and assistance from many people in the organization. By being a *Master Communicator*, you empower people and effectively communicate your goals and objectives, so that tasks get done. Through clear and precise communication, resources required for the task at hand get applied with a lot less energy, miscommunication, and wasted effort. They get accomplished with speed, accuracy, and mutual buy-in from all levels.

What Expectations Are Placed on the Sales Manager?

Finally, we come to the question of expectations. Guess what they call people who make the number, hire good people, promote good people, have a company mentality first, and have high ethics and high standards? They call these people *leaders.* It's that easy.

Sales managers need to be good leaders. How do they do it? Good leaders effectively *communicate* their goals and objectives while they focus on *doing their job* ProActively, and let *their people focus on their job*. If this is true, then the inverse must be true.

If ProActive sales managers want to be effective leaders, they should let their salespeople be *customer-focused*, while they focus on *people-centered* skills. If they ProActively set a culture, become a *culture-creator*, and *communicate* it up and down the chain both formally and informally, they will be viewed as *leaders*. This is what it is all about.

As shown in Figure 1-3, the Leadership Puzzle is now solved. The sales manager's job is to become a sales leader and

Figure 1-3. Leadership Puzzle solved.

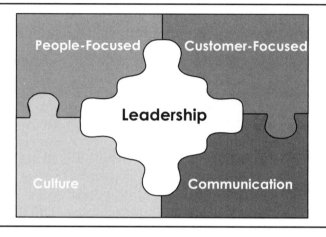

focus on communicating the culture. It is about being ProActive. What steps should you take to accomplish this? What should you focus on? Here is what we want you to do: *Manage the process, not just the people.*

One more time, you need to focus on processes, first making them efficient, then spending time on the people and personalities involved. This is very different from how most sales managers run their organizations today.

Manage the Process, Not Just the People

The key to creating a successful culture and developing effective processes is based on how you maintain a consistent focus and "do the right thing," which means:

1. Focusing Your Efforts on the Future, Not the Past
2. Using an Overall Perspective on Issues, Not a Single Viewpoint
3. Setting Measurable, Mutually Agreed-Upon Objectives

To help you accomplish this, we have developed a set of process tools for you to use at your discretion. Let's get ProActive and look at the Process Toolbox (Figure 1-4).

Figure 1-4. The manager's Process Toolbox.

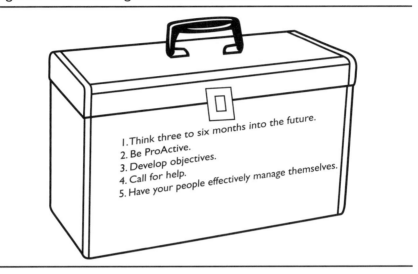

1. Think three to six months into the future.
2. Be ProActive.
3. Develop objectives.
4. Call for help.
5. Have your people effectively manage themselves.

The First Tool—Think Three to Six Months into the Future

It's Monday morning, 8:00 A.M. Quick, come up with three things you can do to effect revenue . . . today. Tough to do?

What you want to accomplish right now was set in motion a few months ago. The results of your decisions three to six months ago are coming to fruition today. Sun Tzu, the ancient Chinese general who lived more than 2,500 years ago, had his notes and philosophies published under the title *The Art of War*. In it, he says that "the battle is won or lost before the first shot is fired." Sun Tzu meant that if he did his homework and planned properly, and if he brought 5,000 warriors to the point of attack where his enemy had 500, the result would be inevitable. For Sun Tzu, success on the battlefield was the result of proper planning. He lived for the future.

This holds true for the sales manager as well. The results of planning and setting objectives three to six months ago are coming to fruition today, either because we planned it to happen, or because we didn't. So why don't we spend more time planning for the future and make the future more predictable? Again, in the sales management classes we facilitate, when asked how much time sales managers spend planning for the future, three to six months out, the general consensus is usually less than one hour per week. This is scary.

Some managers have difficulty planning into the future:

- "I am so busy right now, there are days I look up at the clock and wonder how 6:00 P.M. came around so fast."
- "Every year I tell myself I am not going to work as hard as I did last year. The new quota gets assigned, which is always more than last year, and I find myself doing what I always have done to make the number. Working longer and harder. It's a tough habit to break, but it does work."
- "In between 40 voice mails, 40 e-mails, and the line of problems waiting outside my door, there is just not enough of me. Oh, we'll come real close to the number this year, but I have no idea how we are going to make it next year."

How did we get this way? Why do sales managers spend so much of their time in the present rather than the future? Why do they spend so much time being reactive instead of being Pro-Active?

The Second Tool—Be ProActive

Sales managers are a reactive lot. They can't help it. It is behavior that they have learned over time. Most sales managers were trained as salespeople. As such, they had to be able to react to every potential situation—to the company's needs, to their customer's needs, to their boss's needs. As salespeople, they needed the ability to adjust to a situation at a moment's notice. They needed flexibility to be creative and to find the "solution" everyone was looking for. They needed to listen and be a "consultative" salesperson. Successful salespeople learned how to do this very well. Of course the good ones got promoted and became sales managers. And then, everything changed. Why? Here's what happened.

What makes great salespeople? Their ability to read a situation, adjust their style, and fit their presentation to the moment. Anyone can get an order. Getting the difficult sale, however, is what makes a great salesperson great. Getting that difficult sale means being flexible, situational, solution oriented, consultative, ProActive, and having the ability to adapt. It means using Solution Selling™, Strategic Selling™, ProActive Selling™, and Target Account Customer-Centric Selling™ techniques. It means being focused on the customer and making sure the customer is satisfied.

Good salespeople get promoted. "Hey, if you were that good at sales, you will be a great sales manager. Just teach everyone how you did it!"

Well, in some cases it works; in others not. The real issue is not the sales competency of the new sales manager, but the fact that the management skills needed by a sales manager are very different from those required by the salesperson. Salespeople must be *customer-focused*, and sales managers must be *people-focused*. To the point, salespeople must learn how to react (be reactive) to win; sales managers need to think ProActively to win.

There are times a manager needs to be reactive and situational, but the highly effective sales manager is ProActive—thinking about the future—*60 to 70 percent of the time*. The main problem with being ProActive is that managers are *addicted* to being reactive. That's right: Reaction is an addiction, just like alcohol or tobacco. It is very hard *not* to be reactive-addicted. Interestingly, when managers do have the time and the option to be either reactive or ProActive, many choose to be reactive. They can't help themselves—they're addicted! We posed the following scenario to the managers in our sales management classes.

Reactive Scenario—Calls from Home

In this three-day class, you will probably check your voice mail and e-mail three to four times a day. You are looking for "calls from home." A call from home is a call from one of your employees asking permission to do something or just keeping you informed because they know they should "keep you informed." But calls from home are unnecessary since employees have the capability and the responsibility to make these decisions on their own.

What would happen if, on day one of the class, at the first break, you checked your voice mail and heard: "No new messages"?

You would probably be ecstatic. Your people are leaving you alone and they actually listened to you when you told them not to interrupt you unless it was an emergency.

OK, now it is time for the lunch break and you hear: "No new messages."

Now you are pleased you have no messages, but you're beginning to wonder what is going on.

After lunch, right before class, you check again and hear: "No new messages."

Great! Now you can focus your efforts on the class and think of ProActive ways to use the information you are learning. But is this what you are doing? Absolutely not! You are worrying about what is going on at the office and how everything must be going to hell in a hand basket. This is your addiction to reaction.

OK, end of the day, and you get: "No new messages."

Are you panicked? Well, no. But you are starting to get the shakes and your mind is playing tricks on you. You find yourself wondering whether they are trying to fire you while you're at this class. You're wondering if someone disconnected your voice mail. When you try to get into the building, will your badge still work? The reactive addiction can really play games with your head.

So what do you do? Again, you have a choice to use the time you have right now to be ProActive or reactive. Yep, you guessed it. You send yourself a message to make sure your voice mail is still working and, yep, it's still working. Not totally satisfied, you also start leaving voice mails for some of your people. "Just checking in, let me know what's going on."

You are worried life is going on without you. You are not as important as you think. Tomorrow comes and first thing, you decide not to check. You try this ProActive thing you are learning about in the sales management training class. The morning break comes, and you decide to check and get: "No new messages." You check e-mails and text messages. Nothing.

Now what do you do? You take action. Your own people are not responding to your "send me a message" messages. You are in full withdrawal now.

You start calling people and demand to talk to them live, interrupting them just to satisfy your addiction. You finally get one on the phone. She had to get off the phone with a customer to take your call. "Tough," you say. This is important. They get on the line and say, "Hello boss, what's so important?"

So you ask your important question: "So . . . what's going on?" There. You get your fix and you are happy. You can go back to class.

Is this stupid or what? You should be pleased things are getting along without you and you should take time to plan for the next three to six months. But you can't because you have a reaction addiction. You're focused on the people, not the process. It's time to shift from the situational and reactive. It's time to focus on the process and create leverage.

It's time to put some processes in place—and to believe in them to such a high degree that you can spend 60 to 70 percent of your time being ProActive. How do you do this? How do you start? You develop objectives.

The Third Tool—Develop Objectives—M²O/t

Objectives are the lifeblood of the sales manager. With objectives, salespeople and managers alike know specifically what they are supposed to do. For objectives to be effective, however, they must follow a simple rule. The M²O/t rule. Objectives must be:

- Mutually agreed to
- Measurable objectives   = M²O/t
- Over time

If an objective does not fit these criteria, it will not be effectively implemented. All ProActive objectives must follow the M²O/t rule. Think about it. If an objective is not measurable, how do you know it will get done? If all parties do not mutually agree to it, ownership of the objective does not transfer. If there is no time frame specified, how will you know when you need to take action and whether the objective can be met in the time required?

For example, an objective of *having each salesperson make 80 prospecting calls by the end of the month* satisfies the M²O/t rule, as long as it is mutually agreed to by each salesperson. Without mutual agreement, it may get done, but the effectiveness and completeness of the objective will definitely be in question.

Mutually agreed to Measurable Objectives over *time*. M²O/t. We call it the Golden Rule, and we will keep referring to it throughout this book. It is one of the most ProActive tools in our toolbox. It is how we make a big impact on our day-to-day issues as well as our future actions. How do we start using the M²O/t rule? How do we know what activities should be turned into measurable objectives? Simple. We call for help.

The Fourth Tool—Call for Help

Calling for help relies on the tools we learned as salespeople, so this is easy. As sales managers, we send up an S.O.S. Calling for help requires us to do three things:

1. Do a situational analysis.
2. Develop objectives.
3. Create strategies.

• *Do a situational analysis.* What is happening? What is the situation and what are the current problems and opportunities? What are the primary, secondary, and tertiary priorities at this time?

You should be very comfortable with the S.O.S. concept, since you probably unconsciously did it all the time when you were selling. Since you ProActively created strategies when you were selling, this skill set is not new to you. What is the lay of the land at this time? And what are some of the issues that will arise in the near future for this situation? Do a read on the situation and determine what is going on. Write down your assessments to complete your situational analysis.

• *Develop objectives.* Now, based on your read and assessment, you can develop objectives to ProActively affect the situation. Remember that objectives must be M²O/t. Prioritize these objectives and determine which are the top priorities, which are secondary, and which are tertiary. Then focus on only the primary ones.

• *Create strategies.* Objectives tell you what you want to accomplish; strategies tell you how to get there. Objectives tell you what to do; strategies are style points. They are the way you believe you need to communicate the objectives to ensure compliance and accomplishment.

The S.O.S. Pyramid, as shown in Figure 1-5, is a way to remember how to call for help in a ProActive manner. Remember, Objectives tell us *what* needs to get done, Strategies tell us *how*, and how is way less important than *what*. Focus on the what, and offer a bit on the how, but let them have the responsibility and the authority for their decisions. You have more ProActive things to focus on now, don't you?

S.O.S. Exercise

Let's say you have a situation where you are not pleased with the amount of activity in the sales pipeline. Your situational analysis reveals that your reps

Figure 1-5. The S.O.S. Pyramid.

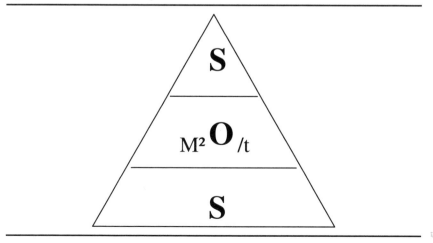

are working hard. They're closing deals, but they are ignoring prospecting. You believe that in two or three months, you will have the current forecasted business closed, but there will be nothing in the funnel to take its place. So, taking action ProActively, you set yourself the following objective:

"Have each rep make 80 prospecting calls by the end of the month."

Now implement the strategy for this objective. Some strategy options could be:

- Have a Prospecting Day.
- Break up into teams and have a contest.
- Have the rookie reps set the pace and watch the senior reps get on board.
- Have the senior reps compete against the rookie reps.

Remember that the strategy is based on your Situational Analysis. It is whatever you believe will be most effective, not what you personally would like to do. It means getting things done through others.

The S.O.S. Pyramid is a great tool, but usually it is used incorrectly. Most managers get the S.O.S correct, but they invert the Pyramid. They spend very little time doing a situational analysis (this is called fire fighting, knee jerking, or just plain being reactive). They spend the correct amount of time on Objectives, then spend way too much time on Strategies (since this is where managers believe their value add is). The *how to* of the objectives is so much fun, managers just can't help themselves. Well, help yourself and stay out of the Strategy area! How an employee implements their objectives is up to them. Provide some guidance, but never tell them what to do.

The Fifth Tool—Have Your People Effectively Manage Themselves

Your sales team and support teams have the ability to manage themselves today. Think about this for a moment. If your people know what is expected of them, and if they report to you on an as-needed basis their progress on the goals and objectives that you have mutually set, then they can manage themselves. Sound too good to be true? Fact is, it really works!

You now have the S.O.S. Pyramid and M²O/t—two powerful tools you have at your disposal to let your team know what the goals are. It is how you set the culture. If your people know what is expected of them, and they agree to these objectives, then you now get to manage a process, as well as the people. There's an old saying: People will do what is inspected rather than expected. With your new tools in the Manager's Process Toolbox, you will now put into place metrics (Chapters 3 and 7) that will allow you to inspect rather than expect, plan for the future rather than live in the present, and be ProActive rather than addicted to the reactive habit. You are on the path of the ProActive manager.

How Do I Know Whether I Am an Effective Leader?

We defined sales leadership earlier. Let your people sell. You manage the people with people-managing skills, create your culture (M²O/t), and effectively communicate it up and down the organization. That's what makes a leader. Additionally, it is up to you not to allow grenade walls.

Grenade Walls

Grenade walls are artificial barriers put up between departments within an organization. They are the result of a failure to communicate, departmental politics, or just plain fear. People lob grenades over grenade walls to try to blame someone or something in other departments.

Grenade walls exist in most organizations. It is very rare to have all departments within a company singing the same song from the same hymnal on the same day in the same church. This is especially true in sales, since the sales department is the closest to the customer, and, as you know, "When the customer says to jump, we say how high?" This closeness to the customer may cause people in other departments to ask themselves, "Why should I change my plans and goals just because of sales?" When these comments start to permeate an organization, you can be sure that there are grenade walls, as illustrated by the following quotes:

> "Hey, it's not my fault. If we had shipped the product on time, this never would have happened."

> "All the customer wants is a little support. I know it requires a Sunday flight to get there bright and early on Monday, but you have to support the customer. It's your job, not mine."

> "This may seem like an unusual request, but the customer needs these special financial terms to do the deal. Our finance department better start getting with it or we are going to be out of business."

Grenade walls have a way of sneaking up on you, and the resentment caused by them within and outside of the sales organization can be enormous. As a matter of fact, it feels good to lob grenades. But that doesn't make it right. It's up to you to break down these grenade walls. One more time, it is up to you to make sure there are no grenade walls, even to the point of supporting the other department's requests. Why? Because of the Two Rules of Leadership.

Two Rules of Leadership

Rule #1. Who do you work for? You work for yourself, your people, the customer, your boss, or your family. Right? Wrong. You are a manager, and you work for the company. It is your job to make sure the company runs effectively, not just the sales organization. Sales touches more departments within an organization and has more tactical impact on these departments than any other department, since sales (revenue) puts strategic demands on all departments and makes tactical "unreasonable" requests throughout the organization.

The responsibility sales has, since it is the revenue-generating arm of the company, needs to be fully understood and respected. It is your job to make sure you create alignment between your team and the rest of the company. You need to keep in view the entire company outside of the sales team and outside of the sales department. You do this by keeping things in perspective.

Rule #2. Perspective. The competent executive has the ability to see things from all perspectives—from the company's viewpoint and that of each department within the company. Seeing things from only the sales perspective is a losing strategy.

Being only customer-focused and not company-focused does not work in selling. In selling, the top salespeople always understand both sides of the issue. They know how to arrive at a win-win agreement. This is true in management as well. You can be viewed as a competent leader only if you understand all perspectives and manage to this principle.

The effective sales manager understands these issues. To be an effective leader, you must practice the Two Rules of Leadership on a daily basis.

Creating a Sales Culture Is Job #1

The ProActive sales manager needs to focus on the culture. Think of culture as the infrastructure of a successful team and a successful company. Why do you think presidents and chairmen of companies spend so much of their time on culture and defining the vision of the corporation? This is exactly what you need to do for your sales team.

You need to focus on the future and balance the tactics of today by being available to the sales team, whose job it is to live in the present. If you spend your time being ProActive, focusing on things you can have an effect on, preparing and planning for the future, and then executing to the plan, you qualify as the New Breed of sales manager—the kind who will be one step ahead of the reactive nature of the business; the kind who will make things happen rather than wait for things to happen. The ProActive kind.

Chapter 2

Sales Cultures and the Ability to Communicate Them

What does it mean to be a *culture-creator*? Why should you spend any time on creating a culture? Doesn't a culture just happen, without your being able to do much about it? Many sales managers feel this way. Here's what some have to say:

> "Besides revenue, what is it that you want to talk to me about?"

> "Create a culture? I am so busy trying to solve my problems, my people's problems, and my boss's problems, I don't have time to even think about a sales culture."

> "Sales culture? My sales culture? It is what it is and I can't change it."

This is what you'll hear from sales managers before they really look at cultures, realize just how powerful they are, and understand how, as sales managers, they have a great deal of influence over them.

Culture is defined as a set of values and beliefs that permeates the organization. It usually emanates from a single person, the leader of the team. The sales manager's beliefs, values, and attitude toward the company, the group, and every individual have a significant impact on the success or failure of team members.

Cultures are real. How long do you think it takes to start a culture? Thirty days? Sixty days? A week? Think again.

Cultures begin with the first interactions a manager has with the employees, whether it is the first speech to the team, or the initial conversation with a new salesperson. Cultures are also partly based on employees' understanding of what the manager's expectations are, and there is a direct correlation between the sales manager's *expectations* and successful or unsuccessful outcomes.

When we want to use the power of being a *culture-creator* to our advantage, we first have to fully understand the power of culture. This power was first documented in a *Harvard Business Review* article titled "The Pygmalion Effect."[1]

The Pygmalion Effect

Your environment shapes you, and you create an environment or culture for your sales team. You have a major impact, whether or not you are conscious of it, on how your sales team does and how well it succeeds. Although some things are out of your control, such as product quality, delivery times, or natural disasters, the key to the success of your sales team is in how you ProActively plan and implement the organization's goals, objectives, and culture.

The Pygmalion Effect is the behavior by which managers influence their employees. From a business perspective, a manager's expectations for an employee directly affect the employee's performance. Employees who are expected to do well actually do well. And those who are expected to fail tend to fail. This does not occur by magic. Messages sent by the manager— whether conscious or subconscious, verbal or nonverbal—have a direct impact on employee behavior. "Pygmalion in Management" offers the following paradigms:

- The identified or "A"-labeled performers in an organization will perform at an A level, and a contributing factor

[1] Sterling Livingston, "Pygmalion in Management," *Harvard Business Review*, September–October 1988.

to their success will be the manager's expectation of A-level performance.

- The identified or "C"-labeled performers will perform at a C level, and a contributing factor to their lack of success will be the manager's lack of high expectations.
- Shocking as it may sound, research proves that when C performers try to perform at an A level, managers who have C level expectations for these employees will treat them in an *unfavorable* manner since their expectation of C level performance is not being met!
- All members of a sales team perform at much higher levels when not encumbered by C performers. C performers will drag down the entire organization.
- C performers can get into a behavior pattern that can be called a "death spiral" when they know they are not doing well and therefore do not take risks to improve performance. Because they are not taking risks (asking for the order, pushing a sale faster, or prospecting at an executive level), they fail. Because they are failing, they do not take risks, and so on and so on. This is why some salespeople do better just by switching jobs and getting a fresh start at a place where the hiring manager, the employee, and the new company have high expectations.
- A sales manager's beliefs can influence a sales team to achieve performance levels that are higher (or lower) than what the salespeople expect of themselves.
- Beliefs indeed can create reality.

ProActive sales managers know they have a direct influence on how their employees perform. You can influence the team directly by having a high level of interaction on all sales issues (taking over sales calls, dictating strategy, going on all closing calls). You can also, according to "The Pygmalion Effect," directly influence performance by the culture you define and implement. The question is whether you are ProActive in defining this culture and how your culture will affect salespeople's performance—positively or negatively.

The culture you develop, knowingly or not, has a direct effect on all sales team members. You can make the A performers go higher, move the Bs to As, and influence the Cs to higher or lower levels, all based on the culture you create and act out every day. It can be as formal as a memo or a meeting to discuss policies, or as informal as a nod of approval or a handwritten note on a copy of an order, saying "Good job!" The ProActive development of the sales team culture is your #1 job. The leverage you can create by focusing on the culture is one of the most powerful communication messages you have.

There are companies you would never work for and companies you would love to work for, right? Most of your knowledge of these companies is based on your perception of their culture. Although you have never worked for these companies, their culture is familiar to you. What is your culture? How can you get ahead of the culture issue and create a culture you believe is necessary to succeed in the next few months or years? These are the questions you should be addressing right now.

Given the power and importance of cultures, how then do you go about ProActively developing one?

Creating a culture is a two-step process.

1. Thinking ProActively—thinking in the future
2. Creating the culture ProActively and implementing it

Thinking ProActively— Thinking in the Future

The first step in creating a culture is to realize that what you do on a daily basis does not help you think about what is needed for tomorrow. You can help a salesperson with a sales call, issue orders, or do account reviews, but to focus on the future you need to create a vision of what you want to happen. You need to think in the future. If you are a first-line sales manager you need to be thinking three to six months ahead; as a second-line manager, six to nine months ahead; and as a senior manager, nine to eighteen months ahead. How can you do this effectively? By thinking ProActively about your culture, and asking yourself:

- What are the keys to success for my *company*—tomorrow?
- What are the keys to success for my *customers*—tomorrow?
- What are the keys to success for my *salespeople*—tomorrow?

As we stated before, competent sales executives have the ability to see things from all angles and from all perspectives, including their own. You must be able to see into the future. The battle is today, but the war will be won in the future. Victory is ultimately the accumulation of your team goals and objectives for a given fiscal year. By staking out your objectives and measuring the results against these objectives, you have a high probability of success.

How do you begin? First things first. As illustrated in Figure 2-1, you need to assess your current sales team culture, your current company culture, and your future sales team culture. Let's take an assessment of the current situation.

Current Sales Culture

What currently defines your sales culture? What do people say about it now? What do you want it to be? Do you remember the best boss you ever had? What was the culture of that sales team? Can you remember how much fun it was and how many positive experiences you received from it? Figure 2-2 is a list of terms

Figure 2-1. Assessment of the current situation.

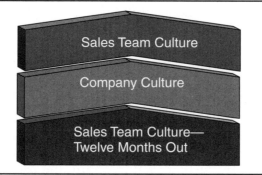

Figure 2-2. Sales cultures defined.

Aggressive	Revenue focused	Fair
Ethical	Orderly	Honest
Democratic	Strict	Customer centric
Company driven	Money motivated	Having fun
Driven	Team oriented	Respect for the individual
Self-driven	Leader	Does the right thing
Diligent	Hardworking	Margin driven
Empathetic	Highly skilled	Committed

that can be used to define your sales culture. Which terms describe your team? You have a choice. You can be reactive and let the culture just happen, or you can be ProActive and lead the culture where you want it to go. What will you decide?

Current Company Culture

Assess your current company culture from all points of view, from senior management on down. Look at the current company culture from the perspective of all the other functions in an organization, including manufacturing, finance, engineering, and customer service—not just sales. Sales is a unique function. It's an organization's only revenue-generating function. Because of this, it is allowed some benefits not usually available to the rest of the organization, such as more liberal travel and expense management, and more flexible hours. Because of these exceptions to normal company procedures, the sales point of view and its value to the rest of the organization may be somewhat skewed. But a good sales team will always consider the entire organization's point of view when it is assessing the company culture.

Sales Team Culture Nine to Twelve Months Out

What do you want the sales team culture to be nine to twelve months out? What is your vision for your people? You need to have a target at which to aim the proverbial stake in the ground that provides the vision and points the way toward the future for your people.

Creating a Culture Nine to Twelve Months Out

A manager in a sales management class was having a difficult time with the concept of creating a future-based sales culture for his team. He just could not deal with thinking about and planning to create a culture twelve months out. His attitude was: "What will be, will be. I'm just trying to make the revenue target."

A group of sales managers began asking questions of the doubting manager. He was asked to describe his current sales culture. He did so in negative terms, describing the day-to-day pressures and the focus on current, short-term revenue. He described a sweatshop mentality, how his rapport with the salespeople was strained, and how morale was quite low.

He was then asked to imagine the future—what the sales culture will need to be in twelve months in order for his salespeople to remain competitive and feel good about their jobs. Additionally, he was asked to focus only on the things he could do within *his* culture, not the company's or his boss's culture.

He described a better situation. He focused on changing processes and on what he and his people could do to make a difference. After about fifteen minutes, he really got into it. Although most of his ideas seemed minor, taken as a whole it seemed like they could really begin to improve the current situation.

Finally, he was asked what he had done to communicate these ideas up and down the line to make them a reality. The sales manager understood: He could make a difference, if only he would plan for the future and communicate his plan.

Cultures are created with or without your input. Therefore, it is better for you to look ahead and know where you want to drive the sales team's culture than become a victim of circumstances.

Creating the Culture ProActively and Implementing It

How do you think strategically and implement tactics, goals, and objectives? How can you effectively implement both your strategies and tactics, and where do you begin? You begin with FutureVision—a management tool that allows sales managers to think strategically and tactically about where they want to be and how they are going to get there.

FutureVision differs from most strategic planning methods. It offers an organized approach to the sales management planning process. While most sales strategic planning methods cover the topic of "how are we going to get revenue," FutureVision is a tool that takes this process to the next level. It can be used:

- In a group or team setting
- By the sales manager on an individual basis
- In an all-day strategic-planning meeting
- To utilize 15 minutes in a busy day
- In communicating with salespeople and senior managers

FutureVision is a tool that organizes the sales planning function. We all want to think about the future and be able to face it with some degree of certainty. This is especially true for the revenue-forecasting sales organization. Because FutureVision is a process you can take with you to a planning session or use on your own, it is a flexible tool that you can use consistently throughout the planning process.

FutureVision enhances the normal sales planning and strategy functions. By consistently using the strategy provided by the four rules of FutureVision, a sales strategy session is bound to take on a more productive focus.

Rule #1: Be the Future

Be the ball. Be the music. Be the story. These clichés are intended to focus the participant, whether in sports, music, or the media. We have catch phrases to keep our focus on the issue at hand. So here is a new one:

"Be the future."

To have an effective session of FutureVision, you must go forward to the future and then be in the future. You do this by closing your eyes and focusing on the future, one month at a time. First, you see yourself today. You then go one month into the future, then two months, then three, four, five, six months into the future. Today is *x* date, six months from where you were three or four minutes ago. When you open your eyes, it will be six months from where you were.

You need to think and talk strategically about six months from now as if it were "today." As you open your eyes, describe what you see. Spend some time to write down what the world is like "today." Where is the company? Who is the competition? How are sales? What is the market? What is the size of the sales team? Who are the customers? What is different from "six months ago"?

You have to be in the future to play the game. Be in the future and look backward.

Rule #2: Think Culture Before Tactics

For a truly eventful session of FutureVision, you must first start with the sales team culture. What is it like? Describe it. Really look at it from all perspectives, not just from the sales manager's, but from the perspective of the salesperson, other departments, executive management, and the customers.

Once you have described the culture you are now in, look at what is different. What things are you doing differently, both good and bad? Are these things you planned on, did they just happen, or are they the result of an unforeseen factor? Write down and capture these changes.

Rule #3: Go Backward

Now you want to look backward. What makes FutureVision unique and so suitable for the sales function is that it asks the participants to describe the past. You now know what your definition of the future is and you have gained agreement on it. It is time to look backward and identify what you did over the past six months to get to where you are "today." What tasks did you accomplish over the past six months? And what actions did you take that made you successful "today"? Capture these actions on a list over a time line. What did you do that was so brilliant over the last six months that made you the super successful sales manager you are today?

The wall chart in Figure 2-3 was created for a nine-month session. You may want to start out with a six-month session and grow to a nine- or twelve-month session, depending on how far into the future you need to see.

Under Rule #3 you need to look backward, for two reasons:

1. It's very hard to look into the future. "Soothsayer" may look interesting on a business card, but predicting the future is no easy job.
2. They say hindsight is 20/20. It's easier to look backward and offer opinions than to make accurate predictions of the future. Who wouldn't want to look backward and predict what they should be doing? We look backward because it frees us from any walls or fears that may prevent us from looking forward. Figure 2-4 shows us what we bring to the table when we play FutureVision.

A sales management executive was working at the world's largest (at the time) market research company. The company's job was to predict the market share and market size of the companies and markets it tracked. This was no easy job. In fact, the company dedicated almost 50 percent of its resources to this task. "Even with this investment, we could only guarantee our customers one thing," said this executive, "that we were wrong. They paid us to be a little less wrong than other data collection sources." Prediction of the future is not an exact science. Ask your local meteorologist.

Figure 2-3. Wall chart for FutureVision session.

Jan	Feb	Mar	April	May	June	July	Aug	Sept	
									List of the future. What is the future?
←									
		List of M²O/t's that were accomplished over the "past" nine months.							

Figure 2-4. FutureVision direction.

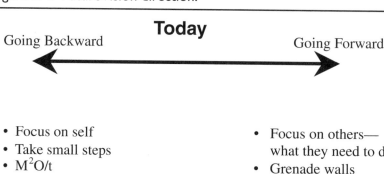

- Focus on self
- Take small steps
- M²O/t
- No fear
- No self-doubt
- No fear of

- Focus on others—
  what they need to do
- Grenade walls
- Many fears
- Many doubts
- Reluctant to change

Rule #4: Create and Communicate Your M²O/t's

After identifying the culture and tasks you have accomplished over the "past" six to nine months, there is nothing left to do but formalize these ideas into action plans. Take the M²O/t's (the mutually agreed-upon measurable objectives developed over time discussed in Chapter 1) you developed in the "past six months" and go backward to today. You now have the objectives you need to accomplish to achieve your vision.

Arrange them into three priority levels:

- Primary
- Secondary
- Tertiary

Now focus on just the primary ones. The rest are clutter and, by definition, not of primary importance.

If you can create a list of M²O/t's and gain agreement from all involved, you need to implement, track, measure, and adjust and update this road map to the future on a monthly basis. Since you have already been in the future, you have a high degree of confidence in the potential for success.

Creating critical M²O/t's is only half the battle. The other half is effectively communicating your FutureVision results and to gain agreement both up and down the chain.

In summary, then, FutureVision is a strategic exercise that applies to the real world of selling.

- It strategically looks into the future.
- It allows you to consider the viewpoints of the company, its customers, and its salespeople.
- It takes you into the future.
- It builds a bridge back to the present.
- It gives you the ability to set tactics "backward," with less fear and doubt.

Rule #5: The Value Pyramids—Advanced FutureVision Workshop

Yes, there are only four rules for FutureVision, but Rule #5 is for advanced players. When you have played FutureVision enough times, you are ready for an advanced level. The Value Pyramids add a level of complexity that is needed in only a few sessions of FutureVision, maybe only once a year. Be sure that you have mastered the tactical part of FutureVision before you try to use the Value Pyramids.

The first level of FutureVision is a very effective tool at the tactical and short-term strategic level. The Value Pyramids allow you to structure the future in a more strategic way to help you effectively combine your tactical and strategic vision.

The Value Pyramids will successfully help you to recognize the needs of the future while identifying the past. They will keep track of the past and the "today" variables you need to be effective in FutureVision. They will set you on a path to a winning culture. The Value Pyramids are used for the assessments of both the company's and the sales team's culture and tactics.

Before you work with the Value Pyramids, you need to close your eyes and go six months into the future. Your situation is now "today," but six months into the future.

As shown in Figure 2-5, there are two pyramids, a top one and a lower one. The lower pyramid focuses on who we are as a company and ultimately as a sales team. It asks two questions:

Figure 2-5. FutureVision Value Pyramids.

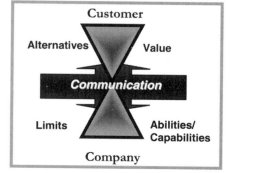

1. What are our abilities and capabilities today as a company (sales team)?
2. What are our limits and constraints today as a company (sales team)?

These are crucial questions. We need to have the ability to assess our current situation objectively and understand what we have and what we do not have. This is more important than an assessment of strengths and weaknesses, because by evaluating abilities and limits we can deal with such issues as perceptions, outside influences, and political issues. Just looking at strengths and weaknesses generally does not take these issues into account.

The top pyramid, which focuses us on the customer, asks us two questions similar to the questions asked with the lower pyramid:

1. What is the value the customer (customer and salespeople) places on our goods and services?
2. What are the alternatives available to the customer (customer and salespeople)?

The Value Pyramids meet at the center, which we call "communication." Here we ask two key questions:

1. What communication processes—both formal and informal—are available between the company and the customer (customer and salespeople)?
2. Which process is effective?

By using the Value Pyramids as a model and guide, we are able to take a structured view of how we can predict the needs of the future.

The Lower Pyramid

List your company's current abilities/capabilities. What are the current limitations? Answer the following questions according to what you do and how you see things today:

Abilities/Capabilities
What do we do the best?
How do we accomplish this today?
Why do we do this?
Where are we strong as a company (sales team)?
What is our current competitive advantage?

Limits
What do we do ineffectively?
How do we accomplish this today?
Why do we do this?
Where are we limited as a company (sales team)?
What is our current competitive disadvantage?

The Top Pyramid

Now look at the top pyramid. Remember that you are six months into the future. What are the customers' perceptions of the value you create for them now? What are their alternatives?

Value
Why do customers buy from us?
What value do they see?
What value do they create that we do not see?
What are the alternatives to the value we are creating?

Alternatives
What alternatives do the customers have?
What alternatives will the market create?
What will become obsolete?
What can radically happen to the budgeted dollars for this
    product or service?

By using the FutureVision Value Pyramids, you have the ability to predict the future more accurately. FutureVision combined with the Value Pyramids adds multiple dimensions to the game and increases the long-term strategic value of the sales organization to the rest of the company. Although it takes quite a bit of time to consider the many perspectives, the Value Pyramids provide significant value as a long-term strategic tool for sales management.

You Can't Ride the Bus

One final culture paradigm needs to be addressed. As a manager, you need to assume a different role from that of salesperson. This may sound obvious, but too often the role of sales management is blurred between a manager and a salesperson. You can't ride the bus anymore to be an effective manager, as illustrated by the following scenario.

A senior sales manager was overseeing the sales function of a $100 million company. The situation was a sales turnaround, not unlike a few he had done before. His S.O.S. (Situational analysis, Objectives, and Strategies) of the situation was that they were not getting leverage from the overall sales and support functions. The people in these departments did not work well together, as evidenced by low productivity and flat revenues. It seemed that these people didn't even like one another. So he decided to put team building at the top of his S.O.S.

He scheduled a day of team-building exercises, which was to start with a high-ropes course, followed by a team interaction and then a final team summary discussion. The day of the event, a kink developed in the plan. The manager had gotten sick with a 24-hour flu. He awoke in the morning and found it very hard even to get out of bed. Calling one of his managers, he explained the situation to her and told her to go on without him. If he could, he would catch up with the team later.

The sales team had chartered a bus to get from the corporate headquarters building to the team-building events. The manager eventually met up with them, using his own car. Still feeling under the weather, he participated in one or two events, but for the most part, he had to let the sales team have all the fun. He was just too weak to participate.

Near the end of the day they went down to the beach, where he gave his sales team a final event. He divided them into five teams and said, "Go down to the edge of the beach and draw in the sand what you all have learned from today." It had been a very intense day, especially on the high-ropes course, where they were up to 90 feet above the ground, swinging in full-body rope harnesses among giant redwood trees. The adrenaline was pumping, the team had begun to come together, and this final event in the sand was to be the grand finale.

But the manager, still not 100 percent healthy, curled up under a beach umbrella and took a short nap. About 30 minutes later, he woke up and felt a little better. He walked down to the edge of the beach, and what he found there was remarkable. In a show of teamwork, in a show of oneness, they had decided on their own to demonstrate they were a team. So in the sand, next to the ocean, they had all decided to build one sandcastle—together.

When it was time to call it a day and take the bus back to headquarters, everyone boarded the bus except the manager. He had his car and he could not get on the bus with the rest of his team. So much for team spirit. He felt he should be with the team and help them celebrate this great day.

The bus ride back to headquarters was one of the most memorable in company history. Laughter, team spirit, and bonding abound. It all came together, and without the manager.

Would the return bus ride have been so great if the manager had been aboard? You know the answer. *You can't ride the bus anymore.* You have to let the team be a team. You are the leader of the team, and for you to be objective you have to get off the bus. No more lamp shade on the head at company parties. No more being in the best foursome of the golf tournament. Be the host. Don't ride the bus. Be a leader. Be a manager. Be a ProActive sales manager. Create a ProActive culture.

Chapter 3

Manage the Right Things—Time and People

Why do we need to manage? What's the big deal? What *is* managing, anyway? What are we supposed to manage?

If you are like many sales managers, you attended all those management courses in college to prepare yourself for a management career. After getting your bearings straight, you were finally promoted to your first sales management job. Then, if you are a senior manager, you rose up the ranks by making sure you "managed correctly," whatever that means.

It didn't take long for you to figure out that you were supposed to manage to make the sales revenue number. You knew that if you made the number every year the world would be right. You knew you'd be measured against "the quota." There may have been some people on your team who did not agree with your management style, who treated you with indifference, and even with disrespect. You may have had a boss who questioned your decisions all the time or who generally ignored you. However, as long as you made that number, the job was secure—at least for another year.

Is this the right way? You *are* making the number and the boss *is* off your back. Why should you rock the boat? This is not too bad! However, is this how you should manage?

Revenue metrics always measure *past* performance. So, if

you are managing to revenue alone, by definition, you are managing to the past. You are reactive.

Welcome to the world of the ProActive sales manager—a world where you need to manage to the future, not the past; a world where you're one step ahead. To be ProActive, you need to focus on the tasks that create leverage, where you can make a difference in a big way.

When we ask sales managers to tell us what they could do to improve their management skills and get the greatest return on the time they invest, their top three issues are usually:

- Managing Time—Where should we spend our time to be most effective?
- Planning—Where can we find additional time during the day to plan?
- Implementing Measurable Objectives—How do we get started?

Managing Time

The key is to focus on the A players and leave the Cs behind. First, it's time to get down to the real meat of sales management issues, time to really look at yourself and see if you are really doing what it will take to get the job done. It gets down to what is really important and where you need to spend time to create leverage. To be truly effective, you need to:

- Maximize your current resources.
- Invest in your best.
- Show me the money.

Maximize and Invest

We will start with maximizing of current resources and investing in the best. Let's take a look at a typical sales team. This could be at the first-line sales manager level, or at the most senior level. Figure 3-1 shows a typical distribution of salespeople, ranked as A, B, and C players. There are approximately 20 to 25 percent

Figure 3-1. Distribution curve of salespeople.

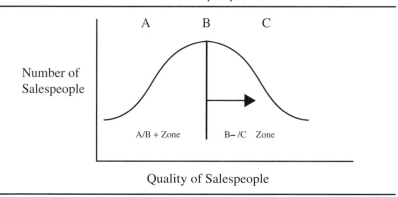

A or top performers, about 50 percent B or middle of the road performers, and the rest, about 25 percent, C or low performers. Your sales organization may resemble this bell curve.

The question you need to ask yourself is: How much time am I spending on my B and C players? In other words, what percentage of my voice mails, e-mails, requests for sales calls, salespeople hanging out at my office, pleadings for me to save a sales situation, or excuses about slips in the forecast are from these B and C players? Probably too many, right?

The Sales Manager 80/20 Rule

In a reactive world, sales managers spend much of their time trying to make the number. They work the deals and situations that are presented to them. Salespeople dictate their calendars. Salespeople tell them who they should go see, how they should help close deals, what to say, how to say it, and to whom to say it. When managers have done all this, they believe they have helped the sales process along.

The problem with this way of managing is twofold. First, it is obviously reactive. Second, the people who ask us for our time are usually not the people we should be spending our time with. Look at your calendar for the next 30 days. With whom are you planning to spend most of your time? Is it the people who are always asking for your help, the B and C players, who always leave messages, hang out by your door, and always have "an issue"? It sure is! You spend 60 to 80 percent of your time on these people.

Here is another question. Why is it when you have those lengthy discussions with your peers, your boss, and sometimes your subordinates about the problems you face, it's usually about C players, the ones who are creating most of the "issues" you need to manage? You rarely discuss what you can do to help the A players be better. You need to spend 80 percent of your time ProActively with your A players, turning your A players into A+ players. Why?

- A players need to drive the sales culture.
- C players, when given assistance, will always come back and ask for more, which often means the same requests over and over. What's more, if you do not spend time with the A players, they will leave.

Managing the A Players

The A player knows there are three types of bosses: those who help, those who are neutral, and those who hurt. The *hurting boss* is the one with whom we do not get along, typically because of communication issues or because we feel he disrespects us or treats us unfairly. Most of us have had an experience with the hurting boss.

The *neutral boss* is the one who leaves the A player alone. By "getting out of the way" of the top producers, that type of sales manager believes she is doing the right thing. However, without feedback and without a learning and growing environment, the A salesperson is not challenged. The sales manager thinks she is helping, but what message is she really sending to the rest of the team?

The *helping boss* knows he needs to be ProActive. He's the one who can push the A players to the next level. Do you remember your best boss? Did you always get an answer, or did you have to ask questions until you yourself came up with a workable solution?

The helping boss knows to focus most of his coaching time on A players. By helping the A player, and by being ProActive, you avoid the worst type of sales management: funeral managing of your top performers.

Funeral Managing

This is reactive management at its worst and should be avoided at all costs. It is called funeral managing because we treat our best performers as if we were at a funeral. Remember the classic funeral scene that we have all seen in the movies, where the mood is very somber, and the guest (sales manager) walks up to the bereaved and says, "I am so sorry. If there is anything I can do, *please* let me know." Of course they know full well that most of the time they will not be called on for "anything," no matter how good their intentions are.

This is similar to the sales manager walking up to the A player and saying, "I am so sorry. I have to spend a lot of my time with the people who need it (C players), so if you need anything, if there is anything I can do, *please* let me know."

A players recognize the reactive manager. They quickly figure out that they are on their own, that they have a neutral boss at best, and that they will need to seek out a better situation where their skills can be leveraged—where they can learn from the best and continue to grow.

Teach Them to Fish

The focus of the sales manager will always be reactive as long as he focuses on the B and C players. By definition, these lower-end players, when given assistance, will always come back for more, which is why they are lower-end players. The ProActive manager knows the expression:

> "Give me a fish and I will eat for a day. Teach me to fish and I will eat for a lifetime."

It is a classic phrase and one that applies to sales management. How often do you give "fish" to your C players? And how often do they come back and ask for more fish? They are not stupid. They know all too well that if they can get *you* to do *their* job, why should they do it? Which is why you always get the voice mails and e-mails from fish-seeking C players. Reactive, reactive, reactive. From now on, *no more fish*.

Then there is the sales manager with the "fishing habit," who says, "Sometimes, giving a fish is faster. It just takes too long to teach them to fish, especially my C players." There are three good responses to that:

1. It is *always* faster to teach them to fish. With the C performers, once you start giving them fish, you will have to keep giving them more and more fish, which in the long run costs you more time and resources.
2. Your A players are starving because you are spending so much time handing out C-quality fish.
3. You need to do something about your C players, and stop complaining you're too busy fishing (helping the C players) to be ProActive.

If you do not spend time with the A players, they will leave. Your top performers want to learn and grow. We will learn more about what drives these top performers when we discuss motivation in Chapter 6. You need to spend time with your A players, or your sales team culture will slow down to the speed of a C culture.

Right now, let's create two lists: one for how to take a C player to B status, and how to take an A player to A+ status. Fill in the blanks below. Actually think of an employee who is a C player and an employee who is an A player.

C Player Go to B	A Player Go to A+
Name: _____	_____
Measurable Objectives/Time	Measurable Objectives/Time
1. _____	1. _____
2. _____	2. _____
3. _____	3. _____

Which was easier to fill out? Of course the C–B Player was since that's where you spend most of your time.

> C–B Player: "Boss, what is 2 + 2?" "2 + 2 = 4, Bob." "Gee, thanks Boss."
>
> A–A+ Player: "Boss, what's the square root of 5,455?" "Man, square root, eh? Hmm, I'll get back to you."

Spend some quality time really thinking about what you can do to get an A player to A+ status. You may be rusty on this one, but time here is well worth it. Some examples of A–A+ Measurable Objectives/Time could be:

- Lead a new sales project.
- Lead a new geographic territory.
- Crack a major competitive account.
- Go to a trade show and find some new salespeople.
- Develop a sales training program.
- Develop a calling high sales script/presentation.
- Pay extra commission for getting a presentation at a prospective major account.
- Lead a parachute drop prospecting week.
- Implement Web-based selling with the latest tools.
- Design the sales website.

It's all about where you have to spend your time ProActively, rather than just handle the reactive requests.

Speed of Sales Cultures

Each salesperson, whether an A, B, or C player, operates at his or her own speed. The sales manager's job is to keep the sales team running as fast as it can go. Figure 3-2 illustrates the sales culture speed game.

By definition, an A player operates at a much faster clip than the others. So, let's peg an A player at 100 mph. We should peg B players, who are not up to A speed level yet, at 75 mph, and C players at 50 mph. By definition, if you are spending the majority of your time with the C players, your sales culture is

Figure 3-2. Speed of sales cultures.

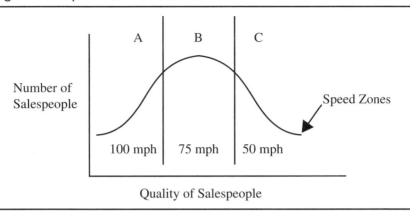

operating at C speed. At best, this makes you a neutral boss with your top performers. In that case, the message you are sending out is that for the top performers to get any of your time, they must perform at a C level. The As may coast, or, more likely, they will look for opportunities where they can learn, grow, and blossom into A+ players.

Do any of the following complaints sound familiar?

- "We seem to be losing some of our best performers."
- "We have trouble hiring good-quality salespeople."
- "It seems the only people who stick around are the C players."

As we discussed, you need to manage to the A performers. At the same time, you need to treat the C performers like you treat the A performers. How? With M²O/t's.

Define the mutually agreed-upon measurable objectives over time with all of the salespeople. You should spend the same amount of time preparing and discussing your M²O/t's with all of your salespeople. Then after you have delivered your M²O/t's to everybody, focus on turning your As into A+s. Spend your discretionary time with the best. Make them better. ProActively let your sales team culture run at 100 mph.

You may feel that if you focus all of your time on your A players, the Cs will sink or swim, and if they sink, there will be no chance at making the number for the year. You may think that the best thing you can do to make the number for the year is to let your top performers perform and spend the rest of your time with the B and C performers.

This may seem like a sound sales strategy, and by executing this strategy, you feel you have the best opportunity of making your goal. However, this is far from true. To quote the popular phrase from the movie *Jerry McGuire*, "Show me the money."

Show Me the Money—An Insurance Policy

Every good sales manager has insurance policies. Not the automobile, home, and life policies, but *sales insurance* policies that help make the revenue number for the year. These insurance policies are what sales managers bank on to offset lost deals or compensate for an individual salesperson's overzealous forecast.

Examples of sales insurance policies include the order in the drawer that you have not told anyone about because it is a long shot. Or the bluebird order that just happened to appear from nowhere. Or even the sandbagging of the number at the outset of the year when you were given the annual quota. Insurance policies are what you count on when you project the month, quarter, or year. All sales managers have them. The trick is to make sure you have enough to make the year, but not so many that you end up underestimating the year. Being way over plan may be great, but it does have repercussions. For example, it may have an unwanted effect on investors. It may cause others to find it hard to meet demand. Or it could create inaccurate budgeting and forecasting for the next year.

"Show Me the Money" proves the need to spend the majority of your time with the top performers. It starts out with a stack ranking of salespeople based on performance and on your assessment of their future performance. Stack rankings force you to rate your salespersons from top to bottom performer.

"Show Me the Money" tells you where you need to spend your time. It also demonstrates that by focusing on C players, you are leaving one of the largest insurance policies off the table. The "Show Me the Money" chart in Figure 3-3 depicts a typical

Figure 3-3. Show Me the Money.

Rank	Salesperson	Quota*	Do**	Delta***
A	Mary	1.5m	1.9m	+400K
A	John	1.5m	1.8m	+300K
B+	Fred	1.5m	1.6m	+100K
B	Gail	1.2m	1.2m	0
B−	Andrew	1.2m	1.2m	0
C+	Jerry	1.2m	1.0m	−200K
C	Cindy	1.0m	600K	−400K
R	Peter	800K	Rookie Exception	

*Quota—The annual quota expressed in dollars.
**Do—What the manager believes the rep will do for the year.
***Delta—The difference between the "quota" and the "do."

distribution of salespeople. The A performers are doing well, the B performers are doing OK, and the C performers are missing the number—which is why they are C performers. Sales management logic dictates that if you focus on the C performers and try to get the delta amount (the difference between what their quota is and what they are actually going to do) of $600,000 from the two C players, you will overachieve the number for the year. This is reactive thinking.

Focus on the A players. You need to spend time and resources on activities that can get the largest return. We have played "Show Me the Money" hundreds of times. The answer is always the same: Spend your time with the As.

Let's go back to Figure 3-3 and ask a few questions. If you really were ProActive and really focused on helping Mary and John, the two A players, what could they *really do* for the year? What if you helped them, pushed them, cleared the roadblocks for them? What if you resolved internal issues and got them the support and training they needed to be highly successful? If you really made a 110 percent effort to help the A performers, what could they achieve? When asked this for all the salespeople—the A, B, and C players—we end up with Figure 3-4.

Show Me the Money—Really!

The results are stunning. By spending 60 to 80 percent of our time on the bottom half of the sales team, we could generate

Figure 3-4. Show Me the Money—really do!

Rank	Salesperson	Quota	Do	Delta	Really Do*	Delta**
A	Mary	1.5m	1.9m	+400K	2.3m	400K
A	John	1.5m	1.8m	+300K	2.1m	300K
B+	Fred	1.5m	1.6m	+100K	1.75m	150K
B	Gail	1.2m	1.2m	0	1.3m	100K
B−	Andrew	1.2m	1.2m	0	1.25m	50K
C+	Jerry	1.2m	1.0m	−200K	1.2m	200K
C	Cindy	1.0m	600K	−400K	600K	0
R	Peter	***Rookie Exception				

*__Really Do__—This is what the manager believes the rep will "really do" if pushed or some focus is applied.

**__Delta__—The difference between "do" and "really do."

***Peter has only been on board for thirty days and is still coming up to speed. As a rookie, he is not included in Show Me the Money. Please remember the Law of Rookies though. When asked how long it takes to get a rookie up to speed, a typical manager will give them twice as long as necessary (another Insurance Policy). The answer usually is "three months." If you ask the same manager who offered the three-months answer, "How long did it take you?" the answer is usually "Oh, about a month or two." It is usually half the time. Just remember the message we are sending out to our rookies when we tell them, "It will take you three months to come up to speed," which is "Relax and take your time, but push yourself." Give them half the time and watch them perform.

an additional $350,000 in revenue. However, by spending 60 to 80 percent of our time at the lower levels, we have left $850,000 on the table! In other words, if we were to focus our discretionary time and efforts on the top part of our sales team, we could generate an additional $850,000 in revenue.

If you do the exercise yourself, you'll find that "Show Me the Money" always comes to the same conclusion. It shows you your greatest opportunity to maximize your revenue.

Are you a reactive manager? Look back over your calendar the past six months. How much *ProActive* time did you spend with your top performers? And how much with the bottom performers? Here are some additional thoughts:

- Play the odds. The probability of getting additional revenue from the top half of the chart, the A players, is greater than getting it from the bottom half.
- The A players are not happy with you spending so much time with the bottom half of the sales organization. They

know they have left this delta amount on the table, which means they made less money than they could have made.

- A players also know that to get your attention, they need to be C players. What kind of a culture message does that send?

"Show Me the Money" is designed to demonstrate in purely monetary terms why you need to spend your time with the top performers. By being a ProActive manager and focusing on making your A players A+s, you are doing what is most likely to drive the sales culture to success year after year.

Remember that it's easy to help a C performer. You do not have to work too hard at it because your wisdom, accumulated knowledge, and experience will provide answers to C performers' questions. At the end of the day, when it is all said and done, that may feel like you have accomplished something. But all you have really done is feed a fish to a C performer.

The A players rarely seek out your advice. When they do, they usually ask the tough and challenging questions that cause you to think outside the box, to examine the way you are doing things, the way the company is doing business. They ask questions that cause you to learn, grow, and even change. While it may be easier and more gratifying in the short term to help a C player, you need to be ProActive and focus your efforts on making the A player an A+.

Focus on your top performers. It makes monetary sense, it drives the culture, it sends a ProActive message to the sales team and to the rest of the company, and finally, it is more rewarding for the salespeople and the sales manager. Besides, it's more fun helping the A players. What have you done recently to make your top players better? How have you moved A players to A+ positions in a ProActive manner? Now you know why this is so important. "Show Me the Money."

Planning—Focus on Tomorrow; Today Is Over

The second time-sensitive variable is planning. You need to spend at least 50 percent of the time thinking about the future.

The first-line sales manager needs to live one to three months in the future, the second-line manager three to six months forward, and senior sales management nine to eighteen months forward. If these managers are not planning for the future, who is?

How can you spend this much time on the future when you have to focus on bringing revenue in today? Here is a tool to help.

PowerHour

It's first thing Monday morning. What do you do? You sit down at your desk, look at your e-mails, listen to your voice mails, and for the next few hours, you are reactive. You are marching to someone else's drum. You are following someone else's agenda. You are being reactive. This should make you angry.

Why do you feel the need to jump right in and find out what is waiting for you? Why listen to those voice mails and read those e-mails first thing? It's your reactive addiction again!

So let's change this agenda. Welcome to *PowerHour*. Power-Hour is a discipline. It is how you should spend the first hour of every day. You need to prioritize and march to your own drum, first thing every morning. That's right. Spend the first hour of every day marching to your agenda, not someone else's. Spend it being ProActive and planning for the future.

First, write your to-do list for the day. Check your calendar for the next week or month to make sure you are spending time with the A players. Check in with your FutureVision goals to make sure you are focusing on the right things. Do anything but be reactive. Invite A players to your PowerHour and discuss their future needs. Get their opinion on what should be done for the future. Invite your boss, another peer, or an important senior-level customer. Be ProActive and own that first hour. Make it your hour, your time. Be selfish; it's OK.

For you to change your behavior and make PowerHour work, we suggest you go off-site for the first week (you need to break the reactive behavior). Go to your local coffee shop, an empty conference room, or anywhere to get away. Stay there for an hour, planning your future agenda. For most sales managers, this will take less than 15 minutes. Then what do you do with the rest of the hour? Uh-uh, no cheating. You are trying to break an addiction and you need to stay at that coffee shop for the full hour. Do not leave until the 60 minutes are up. After the first few PowerHours, an hour will not be long enough. Learn how to be ProActive and how to plan to get ahead of the day and the job.

Five hours a week is all you need to get rolling on being ProActive. Try going off-site for a week so that you aren't tempted to practice your reactive behavior. Schedule an appointment with yourself for about 10 percent of your week. Once you get hooked on PowerHour, you will start to guard this time jealously. Marching to someone else's agenda first thing in the morning will become a thing of the past.

PowerHour. It is a discipline that needs some getting used to, but it pays major dividends in getting your to-dos done and your tasks prioritized. PowerHour ensures you are marching to your agenda, not someone else's. It allows you to take a look at another side of your issues: the ProActive side.

Measure It—Setting Measurable Objectives That Work

The third time-sensitive variable is measurable objectives. In Chapter 1 we discussed how, by setting mutually agreed-upon measurable objectives over time (M^2O/t), you can develop metrics to help monitor and evaluate your progress. By using the S.O.S. Pyramid, you can do a Situational analysis, set M^2O/t's, and implement your Strategies. We will now discuss how to measure time and people. Without measurements, especially without the *right* measurements, managing the sales function is left to chance or luck.

The question then becomes: What should you measure? Historically, the true mark of success in sales was measuring performance against the revenue quota. It is quite easy to measure performance against a numerical goal, as illustrated by the following quotes:

"John's quota is $1 million. He did $1.2 million, or 120 percent of what we expected, and he did a great job."

"Mary was supposed to do $1.5 million for the year. She is running at a 70 percent pace, so she is not expected to make her number for the year. Not a good performance by Mary."

"Gail is on track to do 140 percent of her goal. Nice job."

These are all phrases and measurements we have used in the past and we will continue to use for measuring sales success. The good thing about using revenue numbers for measurements is that they indicate what the salesperson has done in the past. The bad thing about using revenue numbers for measurements is that they also indicate what the salesperson has done in the past. Revenue numbers are important, no doubt about it. They are the final score, the ultimate metric. However, focusing only on revenue causes you to be reactive and measure the wrong thing.

Revenue Numbers Are Reactive

Revenue numbers look backward at past performance. Over the long term, they can be an indicator of future performance, but over a short sales process, quarter-by-quarter, for example, they are less useful. Often the measurement comes late: The market has changed too fast, territories have been realigned, or bosses have been switched. There are too many places for ambiguities and mistakes; too many places for C reps to hide and for A reps going unnoticed. You tend to lose the opportunity to monitor, correct, train, and ProActively manage the salespeople.

We have been talking to sales management about this reactive addiction for almost 15 years now. This is a hard paradigm to drop, since salespeople are always measured and paid on their numbers. Please be objective to this concept. Measuring and managing to revenue is reactive. It can be effective, but left to measure performance by itself, it gives very little information to the manager on what needs to get done. It gives a status, but does little to help the manager in coaching situations.

Revenue Numbers Measure the Wrong Thing

Measuring revenue alone is not the same as measuring the tasks and functions that *result* in revenue. And measuring revenue doesn't really do anything to affect revenue. So, why not measure what you *can* do to affect the revenue line? Measure the tasks and functions that make up revenue. Measure ProActively.

Subjective and Objective Measurements

As a manager, you need to make sure that you are doing the right things; that you are effectively communicating what is needed and what you want people to do. Additionally, you want your salespeople to be able to measure themselves to your measurements.

Some measurements are subjective and others are objective. You need to create a balance between the two. *Objective* measurements, your M^2O/t's, are an effective tool. They specifically communicate in mutually agreed-upon terms what is expected and how you are going to measure the results. However, if objective measurements are all you need, how are you supposed to add value?

By adding *subjective* measurements to the people-management equation. Let's assume that your team has a yearly sales target of $10 million. You assign quotas to your salespeople and hope for the best. Let's also assume that after nine months you are on a pace to make the number. You feel pretty good. The year is certainly not over yet, but you are on track. Not bad.

Your boss comes into the room and does not look happy. You have a suspicion what is about to happen. You brace yourself. "I know you are not going to like this, but the other divisions are not doing well this year." This is bad. "We need to make up a shortfall." Even worse. "I hate to be the one who has to tell you, but you need to make another $10 million before the end of the year."

That's it. No discussion. No appeal. You have worked very hard throughout the year, and now you have to work even harder. What are you going to do? What can you do to increase revenue? This is a familiar scenario.

The creation of revenue has many variables: timing, competition, product quality, marketing, support, and service, to name a few. What does the sales manager have control and purview of? What are the variables the sales manager can adjust to impact revenue? There are only two: Frequency and Competency.

You want your salespeople to do a lot (frequency) of good things (competency). If they do a lot of good things, revenue is generated. So you need to measure your salespeople on doing a lot of good things. Measure them ProActively. Measure them subjectively on objective metrics. Measure *F*requency and *C*ompetency.

The Skip Miller Sales Management Success Formula

The success formula for sales management is simple: $R - F \times C$. That's it. Revenue equals Frequency times Competency. Measure salespeople ProActively.

Frequency

You want to have your people doing a lot. A lot of what? You need to communicate what you specifically want them or need them to do. Here is a sample list of frequency metrics:

Sales Calls per Week	Sales Proposals per Week	Executive Sales Calls
Weekly Prospecting	Executive Sales Calls	Demonstrations
Home Office Visits	Sales Funnel Quality	Focus on A Prospects
Reports on Time	Sales Calls on Key Accounts	Time Management

Make a list of the frequencies you need from your salespeople over the next 90 to 180 days. Whatever they are, establish them as objectives and measure them.

Competencies

You want your people to have a high degree of quality in the tasks they do. You want them to be competent. Here is a sample list of sales competencies:

Selling Skills	Sales Cycle Control	Qualifying Skills
Customer/ Sales Focused	Customer Relationship	Knowledge
Presentation Skills	Negotiating Skills	Personal Confidence
Professionalism	Ability to Get Things Done	Prospecting Skills

The list could be endless. You need to develop your own list of what skills, traits, work habits, etc., you want your salespeople to possess. If you effectively communicate to your people the good things you want them to do, your chances of success will improve significantly. How can you do this? Welcome to the Miller 17.

Miller 17

Play FutureVision. It is six months from now. What skill sets were required from your salespeople for you to be successful? On what frequencies (F) and competencies (C) did you measure your salespeople to ensure success? Once you have identified these F and C elements, write them down.

It would be a substantial advantage if you could put these elements into a document that you could use as a ProActive management tool. Use it to communicate to salespeople exactly what they need to do to be successful. Additionally, if you could use these same measurements to effectively communicate upward, you would gain an added bonus. You could use these subjective judgments to measure and communicate objective measurements. Enter the Miller 17.

The Miller 17 was developed to effectively communicate objective measurements in a subjective manner. The Miller 17 illustrated in Figure 3-5 is a management overview divided into three segments (Revenue/Performance, Sales Competency, Frequency) for five salespeople. This example is a quarterly representation, but it could also be monthly, depending on the manager's needs. Under each segment, there is a list of the manager's assessment of the characteristics necessary for the revenue to come in. They are based on the FutureVision concept discussed earlier. These items, if done well, are what the manager believes will lead to success.

These Rs, Fs, and Cs can change over time. In fact, it is a good idea to change one or two per assessment period to make sure you are always evaluating what will be required for success in the coming three to six months.

There are five salespeople in the Miller 17 shown in Figure 3-5. (This is a summary sheet; each person would be given a sheet showing only his or her own scores.) The manager has done an evaluation of each salesperson. It is a straightforward process that ranks salespeople on a scale ranging from 1 to 5 (5 means well above expectations, 4 means right at expectations, 3 means very close to expectations, 2 means we have to talk, and 1 means we really have to talk).

Let's take a closer look at Figure 3-5 and validate that the Miller 17 is a ProActive measuring tool.

- Jim is not doing well, and it shows by the Revenue/Performance line. He is getting 2s and 3s out of a possible 5. Time to break out *the speech*, the Sales Frequency 101 speech you have at the ready for just an occasion. You know the speech: "Sales is a numbers game," or "You have to be with customers to get customers."

  Well, if you take a look at Jim's frequencies, you can see he *is* out in the field, getting 5s in Field Time Maximization and Calls Per Week. Take a look at his competencies. Product Knowledge and Efficient Resource Utilization are getting 2s. But then you remember he is a rookie salesperson. Armed with this information, you now know what to

Figure 3-5. The Miller 17.

Second Quarter Reviews 1–5 Scale (1 = Low; 5 = Excellent)	Jim	Leon	Ute	Gretchen	Maritza
Revenue/Performance	**2.2**	**3.4**	**2.4**	**3.4**	**3.4**
Sales Y-T-D	2	3	3	4	4
Sales Quarter Review	2	3	2	4	2
New Sales	3	2	1	3	5
Retention Sales	2	4	4	3	2
Margin Sales	2	5	2	3	4
Sales Competency	**2.8**	**4.2**	**2.2**	**3.5**	**4.5**
Sales Cycle Control	3	4	2	2	5
Presentation Skills	3	4	2	4	5
Sales Focus	3	5	2	2	4
Product Knowledge	2	3	4	5	4
Efficient Resource Utilization	2	5	2	3	4
Customer Knowledge	4	4	1	5	5
Frequency	**4.0**	**3.3**	**2.2**	**2.8**	**4.7**
Account Penetration	2	3	2	4	5
Territory Plan	4	2	1	2	4
Customer Support	3	3	4	3	4
Weekly Activity	5	4	2	3	5
Field Time Maximization	5	4	2	2	5
Calls Per Week	5	4	2	3	5

do: Instead of reciting the Frequency 101 speech, increase Jim's competencies!

The Miller 17 will point exactly to the area where you need to focus your time, effort, and energy for Jim and the others.

- Look at Leon's Competencies and Frequencies. This is a good salesperson who did not work a plan this quarter and did not learn about the new product, as shown by the low scores for Territory Plan and Product Knowledge. So, because Territory Plan and Product Knowledge are deficient, what do you think New Sales will look like? You're right: Leon scored a 2 in New Sales. It's predictable. The Miller 17 can predict future and current revenue/performance based on frequencies and competencies.

- Look at Maritza. Retention Sales and Sales Quarter Review are down. This is obviously a good salesperson, but because revenues are down, isn't it time to go crank her up so she sells more? Isn't it time to taunt her with the old, "Well how come no one else is having the same problem?" or, "You are finally starting to become a normal salesperson, eh?" That will make her more productive, right?

However, if you look at her frequencies and competencies, she *is* doing the right things and really just had a bad quarter. Leave her alone. She knows she had a bad quarter. If anything, reassure her she is doing the right things from a frequency and competency standpoint. She will break through and bring in the results again. How do you know? Your Fs and Cs are telling you so.

Here are some additional rules for your Miller 17:

- Each area should be taken on its own merit. Treat R, F, and C separately, since the summary score would be meaningless. You want the salesperson to concentrate on selected areas, not on an overall ranking.
- Do the R first. This way it sets an accurate picture of current performance in your mind. Then you can move on to the C and F metrics, which is your ranking of what behavior you want them to work on (future) rather than focusing on R (past).
- Call it the Smith 16, or the Jones 18. Use your name to personalize the tool. If your last name just happens to be Miller, go ahead and use it.
- Between 10 and 15 variables is the right number of Rs, Fs, and Cs. This is down from the original 15 to 20. Seems when Miller 17s are over 15, they tend to lose their focus. Try to avoid having the Smith 44, the Jones 3, or whatever.

Ten to 15 variables will focus in on the right number of issues.

- Do an S.O.S. to decide how you want to introduce this tool to your sales team. You may choose to give the salespeople a blank sheet and have them fill it out to compare to yours. You may want to work on it together. You may also choose to drop it off in their mailbox and leave town for a few days. You may need the shock value. Remember that Strategies are style points in the S.O.S. Pyramid. Doing a Miller 17 is better than trying to figure out the right way to do it.

- You will have a running score of performance issues over time. Consider this a consistent communication vehicle you are using to inform and gain agreement with your sales team on how they are doing. It is a useful, mutually agreed-upon measurable objective over time. Use the scores to track performance over time and compliment consistent good performance. We have a tendency to focus on what's wrong and take for granted our good, consistent performers—at least in formal communication.

- You are measuring each salesperson to a metric for which all members of the sales team are being held accountable. It is a useful documentation for formal corrective action procedures.

- Be consistent and timely in your reviews. Try to make it a habit. Get together the first week of every quarter or the last Monday of every month. Most people don't like surprises, especially when they are being evaluated.

- It should take you about 20 to 30 minutes to prepare and complete each evaluation. Go with your gut feeling and adjust when necessary.

- When you have your one-on-one, let the salesperson participate. If you think she deserves a 3 in a certain ranking, and she is adamant about deserving a 4 ranking, go ahead and give her a 4. "Winning" will likely give her a tendency to focus on this issue. And doesn't everyone win if the task ends up getting the right amount of attention?

- Customize it. If you give a 2 ranking to a C performer, that does not necessarily mean you have to use the same measuring standard for everyone else. The 2 you give to a C is not necessarily the same standard against which you will be measuring the A player. For example, you may want to give an A player a 2 in an area where you want him to focus his attention. Compared with the C player, however, he is still a 5. Do you give him a 5 because he's better than a C? Rankings will carry more impact if you customize on an individual basis. You are measuring salespeople on their individual abilities and performance, not comparing them to one another. The Miller 17 is the true measure of salespeople's unique skills and the level to which you want each one of them to perform.

Managers need a way to measure the future. They need to be able to formally communicate to both their salespeople and their bosses the sales team's competencies and frequencies. The Miller 17 is invaluable as a communication tool. It lets the salesperson know what behavior is expected of him in the future. It tells him how to succeed. For the manager, it is a communications vehicle that enables the completion of specific tasks required to get the job done. To senior managers, it describes the current state of the sales team, the deficiencies that exist, and the overall trends. It also pinpoints low-scoring areas that may need management attention or added resources. In all, it is highly effective for managers to ProActively manage their sales team to the Miller 17.

Chapter 4

Finding and Recruiting the Best Sales Team

A few years back, I authored a two-day course for the American Management Association (AMA), called "How to Hire the Right Salesperson the First Time." Managers were impressed with what they took away from the sessions. They gave the program rave reviews. Most said it dramatically improved their ability to hire effectively.

The course does not exist anymore, despite much effort by the AMA to market it. Why? No one came. It turns out most managers believe they do a good job of interviewing. Not enough people signed up for the course, and it was killed after one year.

The concepts, however, are alive and well—and available to managers who want to increase their odds of hiring the right salesperson the first time.

How to Interview and Hire the Right Salesperson the First Time

In the interview and hire process, you need an edge. Make sure you have done all you can before the actual hiring takes place so your chances of getting the right employee, the salesperson you really need, not want, are improved. This chapter is about improving your chance of success.

To increase your chance of success in the interview and hiring process you need to do the right things, the smart, ProActive things such as getting some homework done beforehand and conducting the interview professionally. We'll begin with the law, i.e., knowing what you are allowed to do and say in an interview process.

The Law and the Interview

Let's take another test. You decide if the following questions are lawful or unlawful to ask in a job interview. (This test is based only on U.S. law. Many other countries' interviewing laws are different.)

1. What is your name?
2. What is your maiden name?
3. Have you ever worked under another name?
4. Where are you from?
5. Where were you born?
6. Are you available to work Saturdays and Sundays?
7. What does your spouse do?
8. Are you a citizen of the United States?
9. List organizations, clubs, societies, and lodges to which you belong.
10. Submit names of persons willing to provide professional and/or character references.
11. What relative can we notify in case of an emergency?
12. What foreign languages can you read, write, or speak?
13. Submit a photograph with the job application.
14. Please submit a photograph. (Optional)
15. Have you ever been arrested for any crime? If so, when and where?
16. What is the lowest salary you would accept?

Questions 1, 3, 6, 8, 10, 12, and 16 are lawful questions. The rest of the questions are unlawful to ask in a pre-employment situation. We call these the $30,000 questions. Over the years, it runs pretty true to form that at least 10 percent of the attendees in a typical sales management seminar we facilitate have been sued or know of someone who has been sued for conduct or questions during an interview. This number may seem low, but imagine how many lawsuits there are going on just using the 10 percent figure. This is a serious business matter, so please follow the guidelines laid out here. Minimize your risk and ask questions that only pertain to the job itself.

Questions You Cannot Ask

The only questions you should never ask a job candidate are those that suggest that you are interested in information that is not directly related to his or her ability to do the job. Equal Employment Opportunity laws indicate that you may *not* consider the following factors in employment decisions:

- Race
- Religion
- National Origin
- Sex
- Age
- Veteran Status
- Physical disability or other physical characteristics, such as height and weight (unless a bona fide occupational qualification, for example, the ability to lift heavy objects in a factory, or being able to pass certain physical tests such as those required for firefighters or police officers)
- Arrest Record
- Credit Rating or Other Financial Data
- Marital or Family Status

A legal interview depends on more than good intentions. Legality is judged on the basis of the results of your actions, not on your motivation. Unintentional discrimination is just as illegal as intentional discrimination.

The law states you cannot discriminate, period. If a question does not have to do with getting the job done, you are better off not asking it. Figure 4-1 outlines a good application questionnaire.

Figure 4-1. Sample questions for candidate interview.

SAMPLE QUESTIONS

PERSONAL INFORMATION
Date
What is your name?
What is your present address?
What is your permanent address?
What is your phone number?
Who were you referred by?

EMPLOYMENT DESIRED
Position
What is the date that you can start?
Are you employed now?
If so, may we inquire of your present employer?
Have you ever applied to this company before? Where and when?

EDUCATION
What is the name and location of your school?
Did you graduate *(for elementary school, high school, college, trade, business, or correspondence school)*?
What subjects did you study?
Did you have any subjects of special study or research work?
What activities did you do? *(You may exclude those that indicate race, creed, sex, marital status, age, color, national origin, or physical handicap.)*

FORMER EMPLOYEES
What were your dates of employment? (from/to)
What are the name and address of your former employer(s) *(List employers starting with the most recent.)*
What was your position?
What was your reason for leaving?

REFERENCES
Who are your references? *(Please give name, address, business type, and years acquainted.)*

OTHER
In case of emergency who can we notify? *(Please give name, address, and phone number.)*

The Hiring Process

Now that we have covered the legal restraints, let's begin with the interview process itself. There are three parts to a successful interview:

1. Initial Homework
2. The Interview
3. The Final Assessment of the Interview

The beginning, the middle, and the end.

The *initial homework* consists of the things we need to do before an interview process begins. Interviewing is analogous to making a sales call. And as with a sales call, homework is critical. The more up-front work you can do before the sales call itself, the better prepared you will be. The same is true for interviews. There is a minimal amount of homework to be done, and it will not take too much time. A properly prepared interview process goes much smoother than one that is just left to chance.

The *interview process* has a structure to it. There is a method, which can lead to an increase in the probability of success. An interview should have a beginning, a middle, and an end. That structure should be applied consistently to all candidates. The process should maximize both the candidate's and the interviewer's time. The employer should focus on issues that will increase the probability of success, and lower the overall risk. The candidate should focus on issues that will lead to a better understanding of the job before being hired and reduce the number of surprises that can occur after being hired.

The following quotes illustrate some *hiring surprises*:

"I didn't know you wanted me to do that! We never discussed that in the interview process."

"We never covered that in the interview and I'm not going to do that every day. I have my own style."

"I do not believe I need to do that to be successful. If it is part of the job, why didn't you say so earlier? I'm not very good at that."

You can replace "that" with numerous issues, including travel, prospecting calls, product knowledge homework, and a host of other unpleasant tasks a salesperson needs to do. Making sure that an interview process is set up and followed will make you (and your company) come off as professional. And remember, A candidates—who can get a job anywhere they want—are also interviewing you. The more you stick to the process, the better off you will be.

The *final assessment* of the interview is just that: an assessment of how well the candidate fits the profile. You will need to bring both objective and subjective measurements to the process to allow you to look at the candidate in the best—or the worst—light. Any light really. The final assessment is where you gather all your data relative to the position and the candidates you have interviewed, and make both a subjective and an objective decision.

The final assessment is made easier when you do your homework and follow a process for interviewing. You need to look at the results of the interview from all three perspectives and then measure these results to what you are really looking for.

The Three Perspectives

There are three perspectives in the world: I, you, and they, as shown in Figure 4-2. First, second, and third perspectives. The three perspectives are something we look for in every interview.

- The first perspective focuses on I. We see the world through our own eyes. When someone has too much of the first perspective, she tends to be a bit egocentric. She uses the word "I" a lot and always is looking at what's in it for her.
- In the second perspective we are looking out for the other person, always thinking of what effect things will have on someone else. An extreme example is someone like Melanie from *Gone with the Wind*. She was so into the second perspective, always thinking about Rhett, or Scarlet, or Ashley, that it killed her. This is analogous in sales to

Figure 4-2. Perspective overlap in an optimal interview.

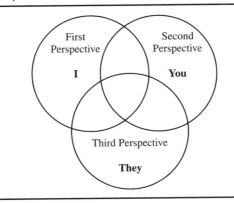

the salesperson always taking the customer's point of view to the detriment of the company.

- In the third perspective we always see both sides of the argument. The Yin and Yang. The Pro and the Con. To the extreme, this type of person becomes so detached from the issues at hand that she has a hard time relating to the specific subject matter.

All three perspectives need to be taken into account in the final assessment of the interview process. A balance of all three is optimal.

Too often we allow our subjective or gut feeling to override our objective observations during the interview. We cannot allow this to happen. We need to assess the interview in a logical and well-thought-out process, and that's exactly what we intend to do.

Initial Homework

First things first, and that would be the initial homework we need to do before the interview process begins. Hiring the right salesperson starts with doing homework about yourself and your company. You need to look at what you do now, and what you and your team want to be doing 6 to 12 months from now, to make sure you hire for your future requirements, not for what your needs are today.

Every new hire is given some time to "get up to speed," and that timeframe is usually three to nine months. (Remember, though, the Law of the Rookie.)

The Law of the Rookie

We always give rookie salespeople twice as long as they need to get up to speed. Better said, we always give rookie salespeople twice as long as we took to get up to speed.

The marketplace changes rapidly, and you need to take into account these future requirements as well as present needs. To do this, you need to look at your own and your team's requirements as well as the company's requirements.

View Your Current Organization and Culture

How is the current organization in your company? Is it top heavy? Lean and mean? Supportive? How open to change is the company philosophy? Is it willing to fail at times to take chances for success? Does it lean to the conservative side or the risk-taking side? What about the sales team? What are the current requirements for the sales team as a whole, not just the current job opening? What will be the change in the sales team over the next 12 months? What will it become more or less of, and how will this change the candidate profile?

Company Assessment

How does the rest of the company see the sales organization? How you assess the current company organization and culture will have a lot to do with how you will potentially hire into the organization and how well the organization will accept the type of candidate you hire. Company organization and culture will be a major factor in the definition of the successful sales candidate. Get input from senior management on what they believe the state of the company is today and what changes they expect to make over the next 12 months.

Companies Change

"My sales territory has changed two to three times a year over the past three years since our company started to buy other companies."

"Changes? Are you kidding me? Since the new CEO arrived that's all we have seen. You have got to be flexible to be able to sell here."

"We have had the same senior management team for the past 12 years. Things evolve here. The company runs and will continue to run a steady ship."

These statements speak volumes to the company culture and what it expects from its sales team. An assessment from your boss on how the company culture will be changing, or not changing, will affect whom you hire. This is a good conversation to have with a superior, who can provide good input into establishing your criteria for the ideal candidate.

Objective Sales Team Culture Assessment

An assessment of your current sales team's culture is needed as well, and usually it is an enlightening experience. To assess your needs of the current work group, answer three questions:

1. What is the current culture of the sales team?
2. What will be the culture of the sales team in 12 months?
3. What are the sales team success factors to be achieved?

The answers to these questions may be more abstract than concrete, and that's fine for right now. Putting hiring requirements together for a sales position needs both objective and subjective input, and we will get to the subjective later.

A good homework assessment of a sales candidate should consider many perspectives, as also illustrated in Figure 4-3.

Figure 4-3. The manager's assessment of what is required.

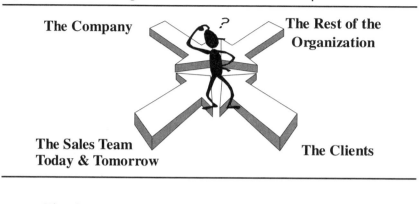

The Company

The Rest of the Organization

The Sales Team Today & Tomorrow

The Clients

- The Company
- The Sales Team
- The Rest of the Organization
- The Clients/Customers
- Twelve-Month Futurevision Assessment

Take a minute to write down your assessment of the above perspectives. You should come to the conclusion that not all of these perspectives are congruent, *but all are critical for the success of the candidate.* How you deal with these differences and align and prioritize these needs will play a major role in developing the guidelines for hiring the right candidate. An example of the assessments can be found in the side bar on the following pages.

A final note on this assessment. It takes a long time to get rid of a bad hire. How long would it take you to admit you made a hiring mistake and to correct the action? Three months? Six months? A year? The typical answer is between 9 and 12 months. This does not account for the lost investment made by the company in wages and training, as well as the business lost because the company did not have a competent person in the job.

The homework we are suggesting should not take you more than an hour or two to complete. Much of the homework, like the company assessment and the sales team FutureVision assessment, can be used for multiple hires and can be updated on a quarterly or semiannual basis. Considering that the alternative

Sample Assessment for Hiring the Right Sales Candidate

THE COMPANY

The company is in a fast-track revenue-growth mode. It needs market share as well as aggressive people to meet this strategic initiative. The company has targeted the Fortune 1000 and based on its products and average selling price it does not expect to get to senior ranks inside its customer base. Therefore, senior-level salespeople are not a key requirement for the next few years.

THE SALES TEAM

The sales team is comprised of very aggressive junior-level salespeople. The need to fit in to the "work hard/play hard" and "whatever it takes" attitudes is important. The team relies on each other quite a bit, since the rejection rate of prospecting is higher than usual, which creates the need to want to help others.

THE REST OF THE ORGANIZATION

The rest of the organization is keenly aware of the need to gather market share, that is, get revenue, and is in a very "what can I do to help" mode. As such, there is a requirement for the sales team to involve the rest of the organization. However, there is a good chance that this may cause some to abuse the company's goodwill or to "call wolf," which cannot be tolerated. The requirement to judiciously use the rest of the organization's time is a key characteristic needed in the sales team.

THE CLIENTS

The potential clients that we are seeking over the next twelve months are in the Fortune 1000, and we expect to make inroads at the manager level. The need for frequent calling during this time is minimal because the clients have a basic understanding of who we are. The clients are expecting us to get in and sell to them. As such, they need to see a high level of integrity and an understanding of their business in order to feel comfortable in making a change.

TWELVE-MONTH FUTUREVISION ASSESSMENT

Within the next twelve months, we expect the sales team to make some major inroads into the client and prospect base. The need to add new customers at this time outweighs the need to start selling more to current clients. This means the ability to prospect and close new business is of higher priority than someone who can get more revenue out of an existing account. Major account development is still eighteen to twenty-four months away. At that time we need to make sure we hire people who can grow into this responsibility at the same pace.

is a bad hire, it is well worth investing some quality time doing the homework.

ProActive homework is a major reason why some sales organizations seem to hire right the first time and some take risks. The risk is too high in making a wrong decision. The homework we have outlined takes minimal time and yields maximum rewards. This is a leverage situation, and it needs to be part of the hiring culture as well as a part of the sales culture. As a sales manager, you need to insist that this pre-employment homework be completed for all job openings.

The choice is simple: Do the homework and see the fruition of your labors, or just take a stab and try to get lucky. Sales is not about luck. It's about improving your odds so you can create your own luck. Do the homework.

Before interviewing, remember to do the following:

- Write down views of the current sales organization based on the three topics above.

- Write down what you want in a sales candidate from the manager's assessment of what is required.
- Finalize your thoughts and write down your homework requirements for what you want in the position, and what you want in a sales candidate.

Where to Find the Good Ones

Now that you have an outline of what we are looking for, you need to find some good candidates. Where are they hiding? It seems that finding good people is getting tougher and tougher. The good ones seem to have compensation packages that are extremely lucrative, and they have those packages because they are star performers. The only candidates who are actively looking for a job are the ones who need a job. The A players can get a job almost anytime they want.

There are many situations where a star performer would want to make a change. Most of the situations would center on the #1 motivational factor for A performers: the need to learn, grow, and always be challenged. They believe that when they are learning and growing, compensation will match their efforts. When they are not challenged, when they are not learning and growing at a rate they expect, then they may be ready to make a change. The Law of the A Performer proves this. The A performer's need for new challenges comes in a three-year cycle.

The Law of the A Performer

One year to learn, one year to master, and one year to get bored and look for a new challenge.

Top candidates do exist. You need to go out and find them. You need to be ProActive and go hunt down the good ones. Where to find these top candidates is the next topic.

Distribution Channels for Candidates

Think of finding good candidates as exploring multiple-distribution channels, either internal or external. We need to explore both, so we cast the biggest net. We need to maximize each channel and use each one to the fullest extent. The golden rule for hiring candidates is to be ProActive and always look. Always look to strengthen your bench.

How long should it take to hire a successful candidate? Less than 45 days. If you have a sales opening for more than 45 days, it's your fault. If the homework is done and there is constant activity in the channels, a successful hire can be completed within 45 days.

There is nothing worse than an uncovered sales territory. Nothing. The quota clock is ticking and the sales manager with an open territory creates a revenue discrepancy that will have to be made up by the rest of the team. This is the manager's fault. It takes no longer than 45 days to hire an A candidate when you are searching ProActively for future growth. Searching and interviewing for insurance purposes so the team runs like a well-oiled machine.

Keep the process of searching and interviewing constant so you are one step ahead of the game in case you need to add a person immediately. This is a major part of your ProActive job.

Begin by looking for the candidates wherever you can. To start, let's look at the two distribution directions of finding good candidates: internal and external distribution.

Internal Distribution

As a sales manager, you obviously have a great opportunity to offer a potential A salesperson. He can earn a very fine income, have a wonderful career, and enjoy his job and future employment with your company. He can learn and grow. So, don't keep it a secret in your company that you are looking to hire someone. Internally within your company, follow these four steps:

1. *Enlist your current salespeople to help.* This is a great way to get good candidates. Good salespeople know good salespeople. Actively recruit your salespeople to help you find good people. Make it a topic of your sales meetings. Put some time into the discussion. Explore options or actions for each of your current

salespeople to help find good candidates for the sales team. Give them M²O/t's to complete. Offer incentives for identifying good candidates.

Get the sales team motivated to help in the search. Ask the salespeople to ask their customers if they know of any good candidates. The more effort and attention you put toward this effort, the more the sales team will come through.

2. *Ask other employees whether they know of any candidates.* For the same reasons as in step #1, the employees of your company may know of some good candidates. You need to post the job internally, but you need to do more than that. Have a discussion with each department head to show them exactly what you are looking for. If you put the time and effort into this, the other managers will respond. Be ProActive and make sure you have addressed all the questions they may have. Give a 10-minute speech at their internal staff meetings to overview the position. Sell it internally.

3. *Offer incentives.* Company offerings of certain rewards if a candidate is hired are always good ideas. Human Resources is the funnel for this type of effort. Add your own incentive to the kitty. Be ProActive. Buy a large-screen TV, put it in the front lobby, and offer it to the employee who submits a candidate who is hired. Or offer a DVD player, or a game of golf at a famous course; or a day at a local spa with a massage package; or a cool company shirt for employees who submit two or three qualified names in a month; or a huge jar of M&Ms (which surprisingly goes over very well), or free concert or ballgame tickets. The list can go on and on. Be ProActive with these incentives.

The results of these efforts will be directly proportional to your enthusiasm. Buy a cool computer and put it in the company cafeteria with a sign that reads, "Find us a salesperson today, take this home with you tomorrow!" Use your largest—and, in some ways, most qualified—resource: your internal employees. They know the company's standards and ethics. They have a feeling for who would be a good fit. You just need to get more of their mind share.

4. *Post it, like you've lost your cat!* Make it known that you have an opportunity, that it is a great opportunity, and that you

are looking for the best candidate possible. Advertise it like people advertise missing cats. Have you ever gone to the store and seen all the posters for missing cats? A cat owner will go to the ends of the earth to find his missing pet. It is amazing what parents do to help find their child's missing cat. There are posters at every store and on almost every telephone pole in the neighborhood. They are all over the place. You should follow their example. Post the job with the zeal of people who are missing their cat!

Put up a "Salesperson Wanted" poster and have multiple little tear-off phone numbers with your e-mail address to make it easy for someone to get a candidate's name to you. The people who are selling cars and boats internally within the company do this to make it easy for someone to contact them. Why wouldn't you do this to make it easy for someone to get you a name? Do you really think everyone reads a job-posting board?

Put a notice in the company newsletter. Start your own newsletter if your company doesn't have one. Send out e-mails to department heads every week listing the unfilled opportunities and what they can do to help. Post your opportunities internally and get the company's resources working for you. With the right amount of emphasis, you should get 20 to 30 leads from internal sources. The quality of these leads is usually very good. Focus internally and tap a resource that is waiting to work for you.

External Distribution

Using external sources can be delicate. But again, you should take the attitude that you are the one with the job opportunity and that you would like to see as many people as possible before you make a hiring decision. Start marketing your opportunity with a passion. Exploit clubs, conferences, events, and friends. Ask your customers for their assistance in helping you find additional salespeople.

Externally, post the job opportunity at the golf club, tennis club, house of worship, or local business networking club meetings. If done professionally, this can come across as great public relations. Do you know anyone else who does this? Good, be the first and watch the results come in.

Spice up your home page. Most companies "list" job opportunities. You should market it. Make it attractive. Ask yourself, "If I were to sign on to this home page, would I be interested enough to make a call?" If the answer is yes, you have done a great job. Use other Internet-related avenues. There are numerous employment pages on the Net, such as HotJobs.com and Monster.com. They are becoming more and more effective hiring instruments. Additionally, there are local job placement centers and nationwide college posting companies, like Jobtracks .com, which can also be vehicles for employment and which are very cost-effective.

Post your opportunities within the profession. You are in a marketing arena now, and you need to announce to the small number of A candidates that you have something they might be interested in. If they do not know about your opportunity, how are they going to get hold of you?

Online networks like LinkedIn are great for finding good people. When someone is looking for a job, they tend to let everyone know. You should have a great network to help find the right candidates.

Other useful tools are job fairs, where companies get together in a local hotel or at one of the companies of like (not competitive) businesses, such as companies in the same traffic circle or the same industrial park. There are commercial job fairs where a company rents out a convention center, does all the marketing, and then gives prospective employers a six-foot table or mini-booth. The flow of traffic is usually pretty good and the cost is reasonable.

Company open houses can be effective as well. You can advertise on the radio, the Web, or in local newspapers that you are having an open house for prospective employees. Entice them with door prizes, factory tours, or free products that you manufacture. Make it exciting for them to come visit you.

There are people out there who really do want to help you, and who will see themselves as being able to offer a valuable service to you and to someone they know. They will get satisfaction out of helping you and the person they are going to recommend. Enlist them. Start marketing the position and get results today.

Recruiting

If you have the opportunity to use recruiting firms, use them. They are somewhat expensive, and using a firm with a less than ethical approach can be very risky. Like any industry, there are good recruiting firms and bad ones. In general, working with a recruiting firm is like working with an outsourced part of your company. You are hiring a firm to represent you to the outside world. You have given it $M^2O/t's$, and you expect results. Overall, recruitment firms may be an expensive option, but they save you time. You are buying their hiring expertise, their network, and their ability to get a job done.

Recruiting firms tend to have their own personalities and characteristics. Therefore, it is important to know the firm and the individual who will be doing the search for you. You should decide what type of recruitment firm you want to use, and then interview a number of them until you are satisfied with the competencies and the willingness of the firm to get what you want.

There are four types of recruiting firms: contingent, retained, container, and in-house (Figure 4-4). Each has its positive

Figure 4-4. Four types of recruiters.

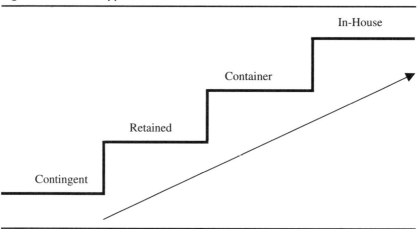

and negative factors. Which one is right for you depends on how much risk, commitment, and resources you are willing to spend to get the right salesperson on board. Here is a summary of each type of recruitment option.

Contingent Firms

These are the most popular recruiting firms for salespeople. Contingent is just what it says: Fees paid to the firm are 100 percent contingent upon a successful hire. This, for you, is the best possible option. No money up front, only fees paid on successful completion. You should pick one, and not more than two, contingent firms to work with. Once they get to know you and your requirements, it will be very easy for them to send you candidates that map to your requirements.

Retained Firms

These are firms that require a fee to be paid regardless of successful completion, and they typically require between 20 and 35 percent of the employee's first-year income (based on 100 percent of the planned income). Fees are usually paid in advance. Retained search firms will commit only to providing you with qualified candidates for you to interview and will not commit to a successful completion. Typically, retained search firms are used for higher-level management positions.

Container Firms

A container search firm is a mix between a retained and contingent search firm, where part of the fee is committed up front and the balance is to be paid upon successful completion. This type of recruiting firm is gaining popularity. With a container search firm, once you have committed to the first payment, the balance is due only upon a successful hire. Total fees are usually 20 to 33 percent of the first-year income. If you do not get a successful hire, you only lose your initial payment. More successful contingent firms are now going this way since it is an opportunity to share the risk between both parties. They do not have to front all the risk, and in return, they either lower their fees or shorten the time frame on a search because with money in hand they can commit more resources to it. In a booming market and with good candidates in short supply, these firms are becoming more popular.

In-House

It has become very popular recently to hire a recruiting specialist as an in-house recruiter. Typically, in-house recruiters are very good at reactive hiring, that is, sifting through resumes and facilitating the interview process. In-house recruiters are becoming more ProActive and are being asked to go out into the marketplace and search for candidates.

There are many definitions of recruiting firms, but most are in one of these categories. Which one is right for you? Again, it depends on your needs. A retained search is the most expensive and the most economically risky for you, but it tends to offer better results, since as a general rule the best recruiters are in high demand and they can choose whom they want to work for. Contingent and container search firms are usually the more popular choices for sales hires. Therefore they usually have a better network of sales candidates. In-house recruiters are 100 percent dedicated to the job at hand, and because of this dedication and the control the sales manager can have, they are a viable option as well.

Fees

Fees for recruiting firms generally range from 10 to 30 percent with an average of about 25 percent. These numbers can vary depending on a number of factors.

The more hires you put through a recruiting firm over a given time period, say 12 to 18 months, the more you can substantially change the fee structure. Retained firms have been known to discount their rates 20 to 30 percent, and contingent up to 50 percent, depending on the volume of hires. Many recruiting firms will take stock options or other considerations in lieu of cash. If this is viable for your company, it should be considered.

A final note on recruiting firms: Like A salespeople, the good recruiters are making a lot of money. Some make more than $1 million a year. The range of costs is something like this:

Retained: The Highest Cost
Container: About 70 Percent of a Retained Recruiter
Contingent: About 70 Percent of a Container Recruiter
In-House: About 50 Percent of a Contingent Recruiter

There are exceptions to this rule, such as the stay-at-home parent looking for part-time work, or the in-house recruiter trying to make it in the contingent or container business and willing to work for less to start her own business. The exceptions are endless. But as a general rule, the best recruiter goes where the best rewards are.

Relationship with the Recruiting Firm

The more a recruiter knows what you are looking for and when you wish to hire, the easier the job will be. A recruiter will take this into consideration. For example, a recruiter that charges a 25 percent fee may lower that fee structure to 15 percent or even 12 percent, knowing it has a five-hire exclusive. This simplifies the hiring process for the recruiter, and typically, the less work for the recruiter, the better (smaller) fee for you.

Interview Recruiting Firms

You should interview a number of recruiting firms as well as the individual recruiters you will be dealing with. There is a win-win here. It is a relationship *you* need to develop because they are the eyes and ears of the marketplace. It is a relationship *they* need to develop since you are paying the fee.

Pick a recruiter with whom you feel comfortable, one with a general knowledge of the market and with whom you feel you can develop a relationship. Remember, from the recruiter's perspective, a really good candidate is likely to go to the client paying the higher fees. Friendship aside, the recruiter is in business to make money. Only by developing a strong relationship with the recruiter will you be able to create a win-win scenario, where the recruiter wins based on the ease of the hire and you win based on the size of the fee (again, smaller) and getting the right candidate.

Advertising

Advertising gets mixed results, depending on what you are looking for and the type of position you are going to fill. Lower-level sales positions are usually advertised in the newspapers. Ask your current salespeople whether they would respond to an ad in the newspaper if they were looking for a job. This will give you an idea whether you should consider using a local paper.

Always consider the candidate's perspective when placing the ad. It's unnecessary to tell readers how important your company is. But it is critical to tell them why they should contact you. A typical ad should address the candidate and ask questions.

1. "We are looking for a top sales candidate who has great experience, willing to work hard . . ."
2. "Are you asking yourself, 'How can I make more money? How can I get rewarded for my efforts? Where are all the great companies where I can have a great career?'"

Ad #1 is really about the employer, not the candidate. The questions in ad #2 are more powerful. They address the candidate. If you want the A candidates, use the questions.

Newspaper ads will not necessarily get you the candidate you seek, though they still may be valuable. Websites like Craigslist also have great potential. Your goal is to develop traffic, and through this traffic you can develop a network of people who may know other people who could fill the position. Sunday and Monday are the best days to advertise, since from the candidates' perspective those are the days they spend looking for a new career.

Prepare for the Interview

With our homework and legal responsibilities taken care of, it is now time to prepare for the interview. The homework we have done up until now has been foundation work, such as making sure we are within the law, and selecting and investing in the proper channels to find the right sales candidates. There is still some more work that is needed before we begin. We need to:

- Establish our objective and subjective measurements.
- Learn how to read resumes.
- Complete a profile of a successful performer.

Objective and Subjective Measurements

We are now about to begin the interview process. Step 1 is to arm ourselves with both objective and subjective measurements. From the objective side, we will look at three tools we can use to prepare ourselves for the interview process:

- The Job Description
- The Resume
- Profile of a Successful Performer

These three ProActive tools will do more to increase your chances for a successful hire than anything else. Period.

The Job Description

The job description document is something you must prepare before you launch into the interview process. It describes the tasks and duties you need to have completed, which is why you need the extra resource. The job description should give:

- Basic Requirements of the Job
- Tasks Required for Completion
- Sales Call Requirements
- Reporting Responsibilities

- Expense Responsibilities
- Time Allocation
- Management Expectations
- Position Particulars
- Territory
- Customers
- Quota and Revenue Expectations
- First 90-Day Goals and Objectives
- First-Year Objectives

Figure 4-5 is a sample of a good job description.

A job description is a valuable document. It describes the necessary tasks and duties. It clarifies in the hiring manager's mind why there is a job opening. And it quantifies the duties that need to be performed by an individual in order to fulfill the job. Think of a job description like you would a map. If you flew into an unfamiliar town, you would want to know how to get around and what sites to see. You'd need a map! This is similar to the job description. You need this map, the job description, to identify the tasks and duties. How else could you effectively interview people about their ability to perform those tasks and duties?

It is hard to get around in a new city without a map as a guide. It is also hard to hire someone when we do not have a job description.

How to Read Resumes

The second objective measurement we are going to use is the resume. But wait. A resume as an objective measurement document? Who would believe that any resume is 100 percent objective? The best description of a resume is the following:

> "Resumes are like mirrors in a funhouse. They offer a distorted image of reality . . . to deceive the eye."

If you doubt this, read your own resume.

Fact is, a resume is an objective document if you read it correctly. You need to master how to read a resume. Not just

Figure 4-5. Sample job description.

Job Description: Senior Sales Representative—A-B-C Company—California Region

Basic Function: This position exists to increase domestic market share of our products. This will be achieved by the development of a business plan for a defined geographic territory covering all market segments. This Sales Representative will have an assigned quota beginning three months after start date and will be a fully functional Sales Representative at this time. The Sales Representative will report to the Western Regional Sales Manager.

Sales call requirements: To make ten face-to-face sales calls per week into the territory. Additionally, a minimum of twenty-five telephone sales calls per week is expected.

Reporting responsibilities: This person will report to the Western Sales Manager. Weekly forecast reports need to be completed and turned in by noon every Friday, or the last business day of the week. Quarterly reviews and coaching sessions to review account activity will also be required.

Expense responsibilities: Expenses should be kept to a minimum. Travel and lodging will be made by the travel department. A certain amount of entertainment expense is expected, and those individual guidelines will be discussed with the Regional Sales Manager. Expenses are to be submitted no later than five business days after completion of a trip. Weekly expenses are to be submitted no later than five business days after the weekend.

Time allocation: It is expected that the first three months will be allocated to product and company training. Additionally, the salesperson needs to complete territory acclimation and training within this time frame. After the first three months, 60 percent of the Sales Representative's time should be in account development, 30 percent in current customer visits, and 10 percent in administrative and training duties.

Management expectations: These will be discussed with the individual Sales Manager. It is the expectation of Sales Management that this individual will become a successful addition to the company and continuously learn, grow, and find a rewarding career in this company and that management will live up to this statement on a daily basis.

Territory: The current territory for this position is the California Region.

Customers: There are currently forty-six customers in this territory.

Quota and revenue expectations: The first-year quota is $400,000/year prorated based on hire date and first three months of training. It is expected that the Sales Representative will achieve the first-year quota.

First Ninety-Day Expectations: This will be covered by the Regional Sales Manager. It is the expectation within the first ninety days that the Sales Representative will have completed the basic training program and have completed the review of the current territory. The expectation after the first ninety days is that the Sales Representative will be a full functioning Sales Representative.

First-Year Expectations: This will be discussed with the Regional Sales Manager. It is the company expectation that the Sales Representative will achieve all set goals and objectives, and that the Sales Representative finds him- or herself in a rewarding and successful sales team.

read it, but learn to read it in both directions. You need to read a resume both *horizontally* and *vertically*.

To read a resume effectively, you have to understand what we mean by both directions. We've always read resumes horizontally—left to right, like a story. That's just the way the person whose resume you are reading wants you to read it. You probably have gotten pretty good at reading resumes horizontally, looking for missed dates, misspellings, and other things that may tell you something about the person you are interested in.

You also need to read the resume vertically and find out the nonverbal messages as well. Let's look at a few resumes to explain what we mean by reading vertically.

Figures 4-6, 4-7, and 4-8 illustrate three different resumes. These resumes are from candidates who are applying for a typical sales position. Review all three resumes. Spend about the same amount of time you typically spend on a resume, and then go ahead and rank each candidate.

OK, now rank each candidate on a scale of 1 to 10, with 10 being the best.

David   _____
Scott   _____
Marjorie   _____

Each of these candidates has been ranked by their past sales managers. And the rank for each one has ranged from 1 to 10. Every sales manager sees each candidate in a very subjective way, which is why the scores vary so much. But when you read a resume like a story, you leave out a completely separate analysis: the vertical read.

The vertical read looks at the *words* the candidate chooses. The individual words need to be read for a more complete analysis of the situation. People choose words for a reason. By looking at the individual words, we gain additional insight. Action-oriented versus passive words: "sold" versus "responsible," "achieved" versus "awarded," "sell" versus "marketed." Read the words for vertical insight.

Figures 4-9, 4-10, and 4-11 show the same resumes, but this

(text continues on page 95)

Figure 4-6. Sample resume: David.

DAVID

Seasoned Sales/Marketing professional with strong closing expertise and extensive experience in telephone, presentation, and multimedia marketing. Direct control of project planning and new product rollouts. Leads and motivates by example . Innovative problem solver with expedient, successful problem resolution. Committed to company bottom line with strong focus on customer service. Adapts quickly to changing, fast-paced environment.

sizeSOFT Marketing   **1996-1999**
Consultant

- Proposed and Implemented Business-to-Business Marketing Strategies Utilizing Product Demo Discs
- Formulated Budget and Timeline Proposals
- Collaborated with Various Corporate Departments to Produce Marketing Copy
- Prepared Storyboards
- Created and Directed Disc Presentations
- Supervised Demo Program Production and Disc Duplication

Princeton Information Company, LTD (Software Developer) **1992-1996**
Director of Sales & Marketing

- Planned and Executed New Product Rollouts: Exceeded Corporate Goals by 62%
- Grew Sales 32% Within 18 Months
- Increased Sales Staff Closing Rates by 25%
- Supervised, Motivated, and Trained Sales Staff
- Developed and Implemented Varied Sales/Marketing Campaigns for Existing and Prospective Customers
- Cut Advertising Expenses 50% with No Frequency Decrease
- Direct Responsibility for Marketing Budget Preparation and Execution
- Designed Layout and Wrote Copy for All Marketing Media
- Guided Company Strategically and Tactically with Product Reconfiguration Recommendations

Chicago Members Exchange   Chicago, IL   **1982-1991**
Member

- Assessed Various EDI to Implement Trading Strategies
- Performed Daily Cash Flow Analysis
- Developed Trading Strategies to Grow Business
- Board Member - Standard & Poors 100 Trading Committee

Bank of Illinois, Chicago, IL   **1974-1982**
Registered Representative

- Established and Expanded Customer Base
- Conceived Proprietary System of Securities Analysis
- Developed Investment Strategies for Varied Clientele

EDUCATION

- University of Indiana - BS Communications
- Computer Skills - Wintel Proficiencies:
  Access   Excel   Corel Draw   Lotus Organizer   Winfax
  WordPerfect
  Word for Windows   PageMaker   Expert Systems

MILITARY

- United States Army
- Honorable Discharge
- Brigade Soldier of the Year

AFFILIATIONS

Sunrise Park District Board of Commissioners (Elected)

Figure 4-7. Sample resume: Scott.

Scott

PROFESSIONAL: **OBJECTIVE**	Executive Sales position in the computer industry, where my self motivated skills and past experience can be utilized to their fullest.

EXPERIENCE:

1/97 to Present

National Research Corporation - Los Angeles, CA.
Account Executive
* Sales of World Wide Market Research for the Automotive industry
* Responsible for new business development and development managing existing accounts in bay area region
* Grown new business by 50% in 6 months
* Increased existing account revenues by 30%
* Experienced in selling to Marketing Managers, VPs, CPOs and Product Managers of major corporations.
* Possess excellent communication and organizational skills

7/94 to 1/97

Dealer's Computer Solutions - Torrance, CA.
Account Executive
* Accountable for sales activities in telecommunications, storage and retrieval systems, Local Area Networks, hardware equipment, software applications and field service in the So. California region.
* Knowledge of Novell and Windows NT networks, AST, Compaq, Apple Macintosh, IBM, Hewlett Packard and Reich equipment.
* Won several High Achiever Awards for Outstanding sales

6/92 to 7/94

PCS - Brea, CA.
Account Manager
* Accountable for sales of personal computer and field service
* Increased sales revenues by 141% in 1993
* Purchased equipment from major distributors
* Implemented and achieved sales goals on a consistent basis

5/89 to 6/92

CAD/CAM, Inc - Los Angeles, CA.
Proposals
* Responsible for CAD/CAM solutions for PC based hardware
* Working knowledge of Intergraph and AutoCAD software
* Instructed training classes and performed demonstration

SKILLS: Proficient on both Apple and IBM compatible systems, WordPerfect, Excel, Microsoft Word and e:mailing software.

EDUCATION: California State University – Long Beach, Computer Science - 1982-84
Orange College-Computer Technology & Business Administration

PERSONAL: Married, 2 children, age 33, excellent health
Interests include: golfing, fishing, skiing

Figure 4-8. Sample resume: Marjorie.

MARJORIE

(Office) 510/555-1122 - (Fax) 510/555-1122 - Major@msn.com (home)

PROFILE

Proven sales producer. Highly motivated sales professional with excellent prospecting, presentation, and territory management skills in direct, reseller, government, and vertical market channels. Especially talented and experienced in negotiating high-margin sales of technical services and products to complex accounts by using value-added and solution-selling skills.

PROFESSIONAL EXPERIENCE

Regional Director   February 1998 - present
More Training Systems, Dallas, Texas
Opening new territory for small ($1.5 million in revenues) California-based training firm.

Account Executive   June 1993 - July 1998
Diamond Services, Colorado Springs, Colorado
Sold and serviced accounts in technology-driven companies (biotech, electronics, chemical, automotive, etc.) in Colorado, Arizona, Utah, and New Mexico. Began and built relationships with CEOs, VPs, and directors to sell concept of Diamond's novel service and establish its value in clients' specific competitive industries and technical environments (R&D, strategic marketing, engineering, manufacturing, etc.). Diamond, a Dallas-based company, provides subscription-based access to a network of 5,000 technical experts; on-line technical and marketing information via the top 50 database providers; research, analysis, and consultation.

> • Ranked #1 in country for <u>highest new sales</u> 1993 & 1994, and ranked #2 for <u>highest percentage of quota</u>, 1993 & 1994, among AEs with combined sales and service responsibilities. • Highest percent of current client retention in country for all AEs, 1994. • Set new company record for highest monthly sales for all AEs, December 1994.

Sales Trainer and Consultant   June 1990 - May 1993
Colorado Springs, Colorado
Developed and delivered sales training programs. Programs included *Telephone Selling for Professionals, Selling to Niche Markets*, and *How to Qualify a Customer*. Designed and wrote sales call strategy, marketing, and training materials for computer company's new service. Researched vertical market for national training company. Analyzed competitors' sales literature for high-tech corporation.

> • Published in *Sales and Marketing Management, Incentive*, and *Colorado Women News*.

Figure 4-9. Sample resume critiqued: David.

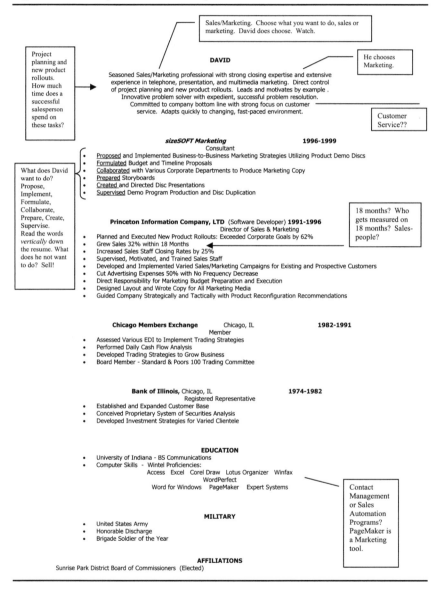

Sales/Marketing. Choose what you want to do, sales or marketing. David does choose. Watch.

Project planning and new product rollouts. How much time does a successful salesperson spend on these tasks?

DAVID

He chooses Marketing.

Seasoned Sales/Marketing professional with strong closing expertise and extensive experience in telephone, presentation, and multimedia marketing. Direct control of project planning and new product rollouts. Leads and motivates by example . Innovative problem solver with expedient, successful problem resolution. Committed to company bottom line with strong focus on customer service. Adapts quickly to changing, fast-paced environment.

Customer Service??

sizeSOFT Marketing   1996-1999
Consultant

What does David want to do? Propose, Implement, Formulate, Collaborate, Prepare, Create, Supervise. Read the words *vertically* down the resume. What does he not want to do? Sell!

- Proposed and Implemented Business-to-Business Marketing Strategies Utilizing Product Demo Discs
- Formulated Budget and Timeline Proposals
- Collaborated with Various Corporate Departments to Produce Marketing Copy
- Prepared Storyboards
- Created and Directed Disc Presentations
- Supervised Demo Program Production and Disc Duplication

Princeton Information Company, LTD (Software Developer) **1991-1996**
Director of Sales & Marketing

18 months? Who gets measured on 18 months? Salespeople?

- Planned and Executed New Product Rollouts: Exceeded Corporate Goals by 62%
- Grew Sales 32% within 18 Months
- Increased Sales Staff Closing Rates by 25%
- Supervised, Motivated, and Trained Sales Staff
- Developed and Implemented Varied Sales/Marketing Campaigns for Existing and Prospective Customers
- Cut Advertising Expenses 50% with No Frequency Decrease
- Direct Responsibility for Marketing Budget Preparation and Execution
- Designed Layout and Wrote Copy for All Marketing Media
- Guided Company Strategically and Tactically with Product Reconfiguration Recommendations

Chicago Members Exchange   Chicago, IL   **1982-1991**
Member

- Assessed Various EDI to Implement Trading Strategies
- Performed Daily Cash Flow Analysis
- Developed Trading Strategies to Grow Business
- Board Member - Standard & Poors 100 Trading Committee

Bank of Illinois, Chicago, IL   **1974-1982**
Registered Representative

- Established and Expanded Customer Base
- Conceived Proprietary System of Securities Analysis
- Developed Investment Strategies for Varied Clientele

EDUCATION

- University of Indiana - BS Communications
- Computer Skills - Wintel Proficiencies:
  Access   Excel   Corel Draw   Lotus Organizer   Winfax
  WordPerfect
  Word for Windows   PageMaker   Expert Systems

Contact Management or Sales Automation Programs? PageMaker is a Marketing tool.

MILITARY

- United States Army
- Honorable Discharge
- Brigade Soldier of the Year

AFFILIATIONS
Sunrise Park District Board of Commissioners (Elected)

Figure 4-10. Sample resume critiqued: Scott.

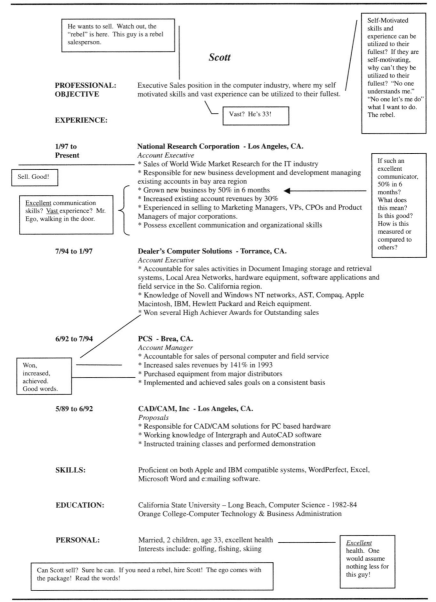

Figure 4-11. Sample resume critiqued: Marjorie.

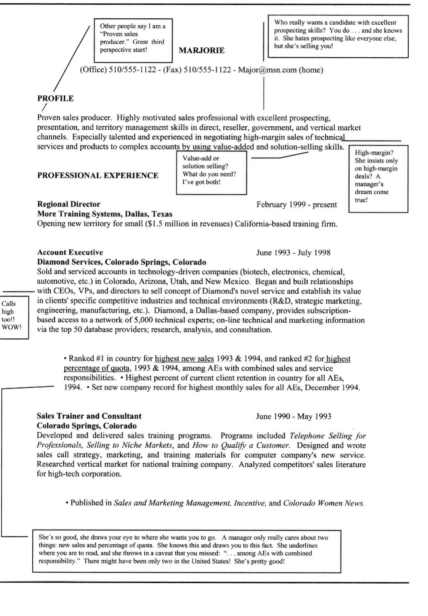

time annotated for a vertical read. Read them again and you may come up with some additional information.

As you can see, by reading these resumes horizontally, you get a certain picture of the candidate. By reading them vertically, you get an entirely different picture. Of course, there are many other clues on these resumes that you can use to get a better sense of the candidate prior to spending additional resources on them. Use both the horizontal read (read it like a story) and the vertical read (read the words) to get a better picture of who you will interview *before* the candidate walks in the door.

A company for which we did some work wanted us to train its managers on how to interview and hire. It wanted to test us to see whether what we had to say would be useful to the company. So the company sent us 100 resumes of previous candidates and told us it had hired three of the hundred, and they were A+ employees. They asked us to pick out the three. We read the resumes and picked out all three. It took us less than an hour!

When you master reading resumes in both directions, you will be adding another dimension to your resume-reading skills. It will allow you to further qualify candidates before they walk into your office and take up your valuable time. Additionally, you will be able to screen candidates to not only their horizontal accomplishments, but to the true meaning of their vertical words as well. Use both directions to your advantage.

Profile of a Successful Performer

The third objective measurement we want to use during our pre-interview homework is the Profile of a Successful Performer. The Profile of a Successful Performer, or Profile Sheet, will substantially increase your chances of getting the right salesperson hired the first time. It has been called the bible of interviewing. Here's why.

Let's assume you were going to hire a salesperson for a New York City territory. What characteristics would you be looking for in this person? What unique success factors would you be looking for?

When these questions were posed to sales managers, the typical responses were:

Unique Characteristics for a New York City Salesperson:

Aggressive	Assertive	Fast Talker
Knows the Streets	Knows the Territory	Knows the Ropes
Gets to the Point	Early Riser	Strong Negotiator
Bold	Persuader	Doesn't Take No
Fast	Smart	Thick-Skinned

Now this list may be true or not. What one person thinks is needed in New York may not match what someone else thinks is needed. Every sales manager can come up with some unique characteristics he would be looking for in a New York salesperson.

Now let's do this again. You are looking for a salesperson same as before. The exact same job as before. The exact same quota. The exact same potential as before. But this time, the person will have a territory covering New Orleans. What unique characteristics would you be looking for?

The same group of sales managers came up with these answers:

Unique Characteristics for a New Orleans Salesperson:

Laid Back	Southerner	Slow Talker
Likes Cajun Food	Easygoing	Well Connected
Persistent	Well Organized	Controls Time
Patient	Good Listener	Cares About People

So what is the difference? Are these lists to be believed? You would probably be looking for some unique qualities and characteristics that are similar, but differences between the two cities do exist. You would also expect characteristics to vary between Boston and Los Angeles, or between a major account territory and a territory that has to be heavily prospected, between your #1 product line and your #2 product line, or between your inside sales opportunity and a field opportunity. The question is, Where are you capturing this information, and how are you using it to quantifiably measure unique job-related characteristics among the candidates you have walking through your door? That is, what document are you using?

You have it in your head? Not a good place. Welcome to the Profile of the Successful Performer.

The Profile Sheet shown in Figure 4-12 is a sample you would complete for every job opening. It captures the unique requirements you need for the person in this job to be successful. Figure 4-13 lists some characteristics you may want to consider for your Profile Sheet.

For you to increase your chances of success, you must have a Profile Sheet. This is mandatory. What else are you using today that uniquely details what you believe are the qualities and characteristics for a person you are about to hire, taking into consideration the nuances of the specific job that you are filling? The Profile Sheet should become the heart of your interview process.

Take your time when filling out the sheet. All in all, the more time you spend up front in defining your needs, the better chance you will have for success. It should take you no more than 15 minutes or so to complete. Here are some tips for filling out a Profile Sheet:

• *Think about the requirements of the job from all perspectives.* What do you think is important in this person? What does your boss think? The other A salespeople? The customers in the territory? Other managers in the company? You may be surprised and get some useful ideas. Go back to your homework and review the unique situation your company and your sales team are in.

• *Think six to twelve months out.* Try to envision what the needs of the territory will be in the future, and hire for these needs, as well as for some current demands of the job. Is there a big customer who you believe will be in trouble next year? Will you need a competitive push in this particular territory? Are you

(text continues on page 100)

Figure 4-12. Profile of a Successful Performer.

Profile of a Successful Performer

Job: _____

Name: _____

Five Characteristics Needed to Be Successful:

Natural curiosity
Complex to simple
Quiet competence
Ability to flip
All three perspectives

Job Skills and Knowledge:

_____

_____

_____

Desirable Qualities:

_____

_____

_____

Background—Experience and Education:

_____

_____

_____

Will Enjoy Doing:

_____

_____

_____

_____

Figure 4-13. Desirable qualities for profile sheets.*

Communication Skills

- Articulate.
- Write clearly.
- Give clear instructions.
- Listen effectively, emphatically.
- Follow directions well.
- Take correction positively.
- Be good in front of a group.

Mathematical Orientation

- Work with numbers.
- Apply accounting procedures.
- Budget projects.
- Read, design, and discuss graphs and charts.
- Work with computers/calculators.
- Prepare or read monthly financial reports.

Drive and Interest

- Handle competitive work environment.
- Manage risk comfortably.
- Take initiative.
- Bring high-energy level to job.
- Be assertive when appropriate.

Interpersonal Relationships

- Be aggressive, tough-skinned.
- Balance people/task functions.
- Relate well to others.
- Be aware of one's impact on others.
- Be aware of others' needs.
- Cooperate with others.
- Be personable with customers, public, etc.
- Manage conflict well.
- Be tolerant, willing to compromise.
- Have good sense of humor.

Maturity and Development

- Be concerned with quality.
- Work independently.
- Manage self-development.
- Handle pressure situations.
- Be responsible to self and others.
- Draw on others for help.
- Work within organizational policies and practices.
- Be comfortable with change.
- Be well organized.
- Be careful with detail.
- Be punctual.
- Be able to concentrate amid distractions.

Management Skills

- Plan, organize, and lead tasks.
- Budget projects.
- Meet deadlines.
- Set goals and objectives.
- Control work flow.
- Have leadership posture.
- See "big picture."

Problem-Solving Skills

- Quickly recognize problems.
- Establish relevant facts and information.
- Analyze problem facts.
- Determine cause of problem.
- Think creatively.
- Find solutions.

Office Skills

- Run office equipment.
- Write memos, reports, etc.
- Type, file, bookkeep, etc.
- Manage paperwork.
- Use electronic equipment (i.e., word processor or computer).

Knowledge Base

- Converse technically about job.
- Do technical aspects of the job.
- Read, follow, and utilize technical materials.
- Analyze, repair, and troubleshoot.

Adjust and clarify these selection standards to fit the specific position.

(continues)

Figure 4-13. (*continued*)

Analytical Skills	Decision-Making Skills	Dexterity
• Collect relevant data. • Logically derive valid conclusions from data.	• Establish alternatives. • Evaluate alternatives. • Select best alternative. • Implement decisions. • Be decisive. • Explain/defend decision.	• Manipulate materials and tools. • Use both hands effectively. • Coordinate eye and hand movements. • Do mechanical operations. • Physically handle the work requirements.

launching a new product, and if this salesperson had a background in this type of product, could sales double?

• *Keep it simple.* Keep each heading to five to seven items. You will not have time to ask about each one during the first interview. That's OK. You will use this sheet to start the next interview and pick up right where you left off. No more second-round interviews of, "I wonder who will be walking through the door, and what was it we talked about last time?" You can pick up right where you ended the first interview.

• *Evaluate right after the interview.* Right after the interview, take the Profile Sheet and grade the candidate: A to F, 1 to 5, or whatever scale you want to use. Do it right after the interview. You will probably have some open spaces. These blank spaces are a good place to start the second interview. Do the objective part, the Profile Sheet, first. The subjective or gut part of your evaluation can come later.

• *Use the Profile Sheet during the second round of interviews to avoid the "He's a good guy," or "She's a good gal" syndrome.* Too often we ask other people in the company to interview a sales candidate for us. After the interview, we ask the interviewer, "What do you think?" We typically hear something like, "He's a good guy" or "She's a good gal." Great! What are we supposed to do with that information? Invite them to a party?

It is rare that someone from outside the sales organization will know the unique requirements you are looking for in a candidate. With a Profile Sheet, you can be specific *before* the interview starts and discuss with the interviewers what specific questions you want them to ask or where you want them to place emphasis in their evaluation. The comments coming back from the interview will be relevant and useful to you.

With a Profile Sheet like the one filled out in Figure 4-14, you, the hiring manager, now have:

• *A single sheet of paper you can use to increase your odds of success and a document you can use to objectively measure each candidate.* Your hiring criteria for this position rarely change over time. It is really easy, however, to lower your hiring standards the longer you have a job position open. A Profile Sheet will prevent this from happening.

• *A way for you to capture your objective criteria during the interview process.* With an A to F; 1 to 5; or a $\sqrt{}$, $\sqrt{}+$, and $\sqrt{}-$ system, you can objectively document your insights and effectively measure the interview.

• *A professional standard that plays to your culture.* The A candidates will notice.

• *A document that reviews all the candidates you have interviewed in a consistent format.* It keeps your interviewees and what you thought of them fresh in your mind in an objective manner, not just based on your subjective notes.

• *A document you can take notes on.* Never take notes on a resume. You never know where it may end up or who may want it back.

Profile of Successful Performer sheets. Use them. With them, you can consistently measure each candidate to a standard you deem is required for this person to be successful. It gives you insight into the future. It allows you to come across as professional to all the candidates, especially the A candidates, who are evaluating you as well. They allow you to apply homework and increase your chance of success. Without them, well, you might as well throw a dart. Worse, you will be hiring B and C people. The A players are going to go to the companies that have their act together. The ones that come off as professional

Figure 4-14. Completed profile sheet of a successful performer.

Profile of a Successful Performer

Job: Sales Representative: ABC Company—Northeast Territory

Name: _____

Five Characteristics Needed to Be Successful:

Natural curiosity
Complex to simple
Quiet competence
Ability to flip
All three perspectives

Job Skills and Knowledge:

Wants to make a difference
Sales—successful/unsuccessful/successful
Sales management
Well connected in the industry
Can entertain and educate

Desirable Qualities:

Persistence
Call at the top
Empathy—puts the customer first
Carries herself well
Self-motivated
Makes sacrifices

Background—Experience and Education:

Five to seven years relative sales experience
Four-year degree
Multiple industries
Product XYZ experience
Desire to work with others

Will Enjoy Doing:

Being on her own
Getting up in the morning
Learning and growing
Helping customers
Being a part of a team—no lone wolves
Having choice, not freedom

during the interview. The ones that are ProActive and are using Profile Sheets.

The Interview Process

The overall process of interviewing should:

- Allow the employer the opportunity to evaluate for the best possible hire, based on the information on the Profile Sheet.
- Allow the candidate to evaluate the opportunity and determine whether she wants to work for the employer.
- Ensure a mutual cultural fit.

These objectives can be accomplished by an interview process we call the A-B-C interview process.

The A-B-C Interview Process

Now that you have defined how to measure the interview with Profile Sheets, let's look at a process that allows you, the hiring manager, to look at as many candidates as possible in a definitive time frame. This is the A-B-C interview process, which, as the name implies, is divided into three segments: Rounds A, B, and C.

Round A

See the world. Your first initial interviews in Round A allow you to view as many candidates as possible within a certain time frame. For example, you decide that between now and the end of July you will hold Round A interviews. Set yourself some measurable objectives ($M^2O/t's$) to make sure you accomplish this goal. Round A interviews should be approximately 20 to 30 minutes in duration, and candidates should be told this up front. This allows you time to hold as many Round A interviews as possible and additionally sets the time expectation right up front with the candidate. But be flexible. End an interview after 20 minutes if it is not going well, but allow 30 to 40 minutes for a very good candidate. Stating the time frame up front allows you flexibility on how to end the interview.

The initial Round A interview can be in person or over the phone, because both fulfill the same objective. Over time and armed with intuition you will be able to determine whether the candidate meets your criteria.

An interview should be conducted in a natural setting. If interviewing in person, in your office, don't sit behind your desk, but around a table. Cafeterias, airport lounges, and restaurants are good places for interviews. It should be a comfortable area where you can put the candidate at ease and have a private discussion. The golden rule is never, ever, ever, ever interview a candidate in a hotel room. It does not matter whether you have a suite, where the bedroom is a separate room. You never know what someone may be willing to say happened or what they may actually do behind closed doors.

Try to interview in the morning and interview as early in the week as possible. The pressures of the day seem to mount in the afternoon and later in the week. Early-morning interviews between 7:00 A.M. and 8:00 A.M. work well, but an interview after 6:00 P.M. may not put you or the candidate in the best possible mental state.

By the end of Round A, you will know which candidates go on to Round B. Typically between one and three candidates will make the grade.

Round B

In Round B, other people in the organization are now interviewing your top candidates. This round should last between one and three weeks. Arm the other interviewers with your objective interviewing criteria, such as resume, job description, and Profile Sheet. Review these metrics with each interviewer and point out significant areas you want them to concentrate on. This will provide you with favorable feedback and avoid the "good guy/good gal" scenario.

Round C

Round C is the final interview. Take the candidate off-site with other salespeople or other people in your company for a subjective interview. Now is the time you should evaluate how well the candidate will fit into your sales team culture. The chemistry of the sales team requires that all members interact with and leverage off of one another whenever possible. A culture match is important.

Round C should be held at lunch or after work at a local restaurant or cafe. If this is not possible because the candidate is at a remote location, have the candidate spend time with a remote salesperson. You need to evaluate the culture fit outside of the controlled office environment. Round C interviews are very important. Many sales managers have disqualified candidates in the final round, even though they looked strong in Rounds A and B.

Summary

Typically, the A-B-C interview process timeline looks like this:

Round A	1 to 4 weeks
Round B	1 to 3 weeks
Round C	1 to 2 weeks
Total Time	3 to 9 weeks

This is the total elapsed time per candidate. It is possible to have multiple candidates hire on during this three- to nine-week schedule. Overlapping hires is a normal process. However, each candidate should be put through the A-B-C process.

What happens if you find a "perfect" candidate and her timeline is not the same as yours? Should you tell the candidate, "Sorry, I am taking to the end of the month to evaluate all potential candidates, and if you cannot adapt to this schedule, there is nothing I can do"? Of course not. If this happens with a top candidate, who for some outside reason needs to make a decision in a time frame that is not consistent with yours, you can do one of two things:

1. Dismiss the candidate, saying you are not going to compromise the process.
2. Run the candidate through a special interview process.

Most sales managers would select option 2. Just make sure you know the risks you are taking. By treating this candidate in a special manner, you may be putting yourself in a less than optimal negotiating position. You have also stopped the interviewing process, and if this candidate does not work out, it will cost you something (time) to start the process back up again. If you are going to make a decision to shorten the process, make sure you evaluate the risks before you do it. Discuss with the candidate what you are going to do for them. Gain their agreement that if the accelerated process works out, they will be in a position to accept an offer if one is appropriate. In other words, qualify the heck out of the candidate to minimize your risk.

Your objective is to hire the best candidate available and use time as an ally. The A-B-C process will filter the right candidate through the process to increase your chance of making the right decision.

The Twenty-Minute Interview Process

How long are your first-round interviews? Usually about 40 to 60 minutes? How long are your first-round interviews with those "C" candidates? The ones where you know in the first 10 minutes that you should call it off, but you give them the full hour because it is the right thing to do? Time to change. Welcome to an interview process that will allow you to:

- Stay in control of the interview.
- Make the most out of the time allocated.
- Make the most out of the two-way communication between the candidate and yourself.
- Allow you flexibility when interviewing an A candidate.
- Get rid of the C candidates in 20 minutes or less.

A Simple but Effective Interview Process: Connect-Draw-Give-Close

Now that we have discussed the strategy of the interview process, let's get down to tactics. In the interview process, the goal is an efficient and effective interview. Have great interviews with top candidates, and get the C candidates out the door in a time-efficient but professional manner. You want to be able to maximize the time you are spending with each candidate, a lot with the good ones and a little with the not-so-good ones.

To do this, you must have control of the interview so you can evaluate what your next step should be. Should you talk first or have the candidate talk first? What ratio of talk/listen is effective? Who should be talking at the end? The interview process Connect-Draw-Give-Close can address these questions.

Connect-Draw-Give-Close is a four-step process that, when followed, can guide a manager to a productive and efficient interview. The process has been designed to allow you the most flexibility to gather important information, while allowing a structure to be put into place for consistency during interviews. The first step is Connect.

Step 1: Connect

Connect with the interviewee, develop rapport, and de-stress the candidate. Create a comfortable situation so that information can flow efficiently by using connect starters:

"Good morning. May I get you a glass of water or a cup of coffee?"

"Hello. Did you have any trouble finding the building?"

"Good morning. How has your day been?"

These are typical de-stressing questions with which to start the interview before getting into the process. Give the candidate time to breathe and relax. Connect with the candidate and build rapport.

This is also part of the interview where you set up the time frame expectations for the interview by saying something like:

"OK, thanks for coming. We usually allocate about 20 to 30 minutes for first-round interviews. This maximizes both your time and mine, and it sets the stage for future interviews, if appropriate. With that said, let's get started."

With a beginning statement like this, you have set the stage for the interview to last no more than 20 to 30 minutes. If the candidate is not a fit, you can dismiss the candidate in 20 minutes. If the candidate is a good one, and *you* want the conversation to last longer, you can. It's your choice. This is how you can maximize your time, by stating the time requirements up front, then choosing how long you want the interview to last. No more 60-minute C interviews. If you have been spending 40 to 60 minutes interviewing C candidates, this tool alone is worth the price of admission.

Step 2: Draw

Now it's time to draw information out. Before you give the candidate a lot of information, draw as much as you can from the candidate to determine his current position and fit. This will allow you to determine how much longer you want to spend with this candidate, based on the time frame you set up in the connect process. If within the first 10 minutes you feel this candidate has potential, then continue to draw out as much as possible. After 20 to 30 minutes, go to the Give phase. If he is not a good candidate, stop the Draw phase after 10 minutes or so and go to the Give phase, albeit a short one since it's unlikely you will hire this candidate.

Remember the second step is Draw. The natural tendency is for the sales manager to want to have control of the interview and give at first, to hurry things along with a C candidate, and start selling an A candidate. *The second step is Draw.* Especially for the A candidate. Stop selling and start listening so you can control the interview and win the candidate over. Let him talk first. This was effective when you were a salesperson. Same thing.

Step 3: Give

You are in control of the interview. Now is the time to give the candidate information about the position and the company, especially to a top candidate. Now is not the time to oversell; just keep the process of Draw and Give going for a while longer. A top candidate will be trying to get control of the interview anyway, so a good back and forth (Draw and Give) conversation is a positive outcome.

You also have the ability to shorten the amount of information you give to a candidate if your initial assessment does not indicate a fit, and wrap this interview up in 20 to 30 minutes. Why spend time prolonging the interview, telling the candidate all about the company and the position if you already decided against hiring her? Shorten the Give content amount and proceed to the next step.

Step 4: Close

This step is a natural summation of the conversation described in the A-B-C interview process. The close is very important because it provides you with the opportunity to:

- Shorten or lengthen the interview based on the quality of the interview.
- Assess the candidate's reaction to the interview.
- Make the candidate feel that she is involved with a professional organization.

Finish the interview by describing the A-B-C interview process, and then wrapping it up. This will allow you to avoid the candidate's "How did I do" type of questions usually asked at the end of the interview, which can be hard to get out of. These questions can be especially awkward with a C candidate, so reviewing the A-B-C process with the candidate at the end will allow you to honestly say you are not actually judging candidates at this time. All you are doing is collecting Profile Sheets; the ranking or judging of candidates will come later in the process. Here is an example of such a close:

> *Manager:* "Thanks for coming. We are right now in Round A of the interview process, and we expect to finish this round by the end of the month, then assess the situation and ask a few candidates back if appropriate."
> *Candidate:* "So how did I do? How do I stack up against who you have seen so far?"
> *Manager:* "Well, we are really not measuring individual candidates against one another. At the end of Round A we will evaluate all the candidates against our profile and make a decision at that point. So I really can't tell you how you did, because we just do not evaluate that way. Thanks for coming though, and if appropriate, we'll be in touch."

Connect-Draw-Give-Close is a four-step interview process that works. It keeps you in charge, allows you to assess the candidate fairly, and lets you control the time spent in the interview. It comes across as professional to the candidate, and it allows you to organize the interview flow to your advantage.

Interview—Sales Call

Why do so many sales managers treat an interview like an interview? It is because they have been shown and been involved with so many interviews, that they assume they know how to interview effectively. The sales manager asks the questions, and the candidate answers the questions. We drill the candidate on items in the resume, and the candidate answers. We finish up the interview by saying we'll be in touch. The candidate leaves. How tough is this really?

Well, there is a better way. The interview process is a communication between two people. Both may have something the other side wants. Both are evaluating each other to determine whether they want to create a relationship. Both are hoping their needs can be satisfied in this meeting. They are selling to each other. The sales manager is selling the company and the position. The candidate is selling himself and his qualifications and experience. So why do we treat the interview like an interview? Why not treat the interview like a selling situation, which it is, and evaluate the candidate's sales ability?

Treat the Interview Like a Sales Call

"I've just never thought about treating the interview like a sales call. I've always been told it's our job to uncover who is sitting across from you, and that's about it."

"I've always been too busy asking my questions and listening to the answers to even think during the interview to evaluate their sales ability."

"Interview—sales call, sales call—interview. Treat the interview like a sales call. What a refreshing approach."

By treating the interview like a sales call, you will be evaluating for competent and success-related sales qualities. You will be looking for how well the sales candidates can actually sell themselves—a novel, yet effective idea.

By treating the interview like a sales call, you naturally create a win-win relationship. Both parties have a stake in the game. They are evaluating each other to determine needs and to see whether the needs can be satisfied. Each party hopes the other one has an answer to their own individual needs and will "pay" for a solution. This *is* a sales call, so let's treat it as such. Figure 4-15 lists the advantages of treating an interview like a sales call.

So, if looking at an interview as a sales call is a good tool to use in an interview, what other tools can a ProActive sales manager use in an interview—or, rather, a sales call/interview?

Tools for the Sales Interview

During the interview, the sales manager should be looking for the candidate to demonstrate some selling skills. The first thing a candidate should try to do is control the interview like a salesperson would control a sales call. This is exactly what a sales manager is looking for when she goes on sales calls with her

Figure 4-15. Advantages of treating an interview like a sales call.

	Treat Like Interview	*Treat Like Sales Call*
Objective	Make Decision (Y/N)	Evaluate Sales Ability
Responsibility	Individualistic	Mutual Goals
Time Constraints	Make Decision Now	Work the Process
Approach	Us vs. Them	Collaborative
Direction	One Way	Two Way
Needs Satisfied	Own Benefit	Mutual Benefit
Process	Situational	Evaluative
Climate	Pressure to Perform	Mutual Win-Win

current sales team. Does the salesperson take control of the sales call? Evaluate the same qualities during the interview process. Other selling skill attributes during the interview to look for include:

• *Analogies.* Great salespeople are great storytellers. They can relate to their customers and empathize with them through stories and analogies. Watch for the stories to come out during the interview. Observe whether the candidate can sum up some points of the conversation with a story. If she does this in an interview, she is going to do it on a sales call.

• *Focused with a Purpose.* Are their stories focused and do they have a purpose? Are they crisp? Do they have a beginning, middle, and an end? Do they go off into la-la land or do the stories relate to the topic at hand? Are you sitting there during the interview asking yourself, "What is the point of this story?" Do the candidates find themselves at a loss and ask, "Where were we?" or "What's the question?" Many sales managers have been on those sales calls when they ask themselves, "Does this salesperson have a clue where she is headed with this conversation?" Most times the sales manager has to jump in and put the sales call back on track. If the candidate goes off track in the interview, she'll do it on a sales call.

• *Who Starts Round 2?* During most interviews, following the initial five- to ten-second rapport time (which we'll call Round 1), you as the interviewer should pause, for about five seconds. Allow the candidate to take control of the interview. We call the time after the pause Round 2. We are always looking for the salesperson to take control of a sales call, so why should this be any different? For example:

> *Manager:* "Good morning, can I get you a cup of coffee or a glass of water?"
> *Candidate:* "No thanks, just had two cups already this morning."
> *Manager:* "No problem. Please have a seat."

At this point, pause the conversation for a few seconds. This is the transition from Round 1, the opening to Round 2, the heart of the interview. Watch and see whether the sales candidate takes control of this call/interview.

> *Example #1* (after an approximate three-second pause)
> *Candidate:* "Thanks for inviting me in today. I have done a little homework on the company, and if it is OK with you, I have some questions I would like to get answered sometime during this interview. Would now be a good time?"

> *Example #2* (after a four- to five-second pause)
> *Manager:* "Let's get started. Please tell me about yourself and your recent accomplishments."

It's obvious that in Example #1 the sales candidate took control of this sales interview, and if she shows this skill in the interview, she will have it on a sales call. In Example #2, the manager had to take control. Look for this skill by giving the candidate the opportunity to start Round 2.

• *Who Takes Control?* You as the manager have total control of the sales interview. You're the one with the job to fill, so you have total control. So give it up. Give up control of the interview to the sales candidate who wants it, who asks for it, who just takes it. In Example #1, the manager should feel comfortable answering the candidate:

Manager: "Now is a good time. What questions do you have?"

Observe whether the candidate is well organized and asks pertinent questions. The candidate has asked for control of this sales call/interview, so evaluate her ability to control it and what she actually does with it. How well does she handle the questioning and the listening part of the sales interview? These control skills are something you are looking for in a salesperson, and these skills will come out during the interview.

You have the control of the interview with *Connect-Draw-Give-Close,* so give control to the sales candidate who "asks" for it. If they have the skill to control a sales interview, they can control a sales call.

• *Flip.* The art of the flip. Great salespeople are great flippers. Wouldn't you agree? (You have just been flipped.) Flipping is a salesperson's tool. It is a way to get the "buyer" to talk, and in the case of the sales interview, the "buyer" is you, the sales manager. Flipping is a sales tool we teach in "ProActive Selling," our sales training course. A great salesperson knows when to flip and get the buyer involved.

Flip Example
Buyer: "So Jack, tell me why you are interested in coming to work for us."
Jack: "Sure. I have seven years of sales experience, five in your current industry. . . ." (A seven- to eight-minute story of blah, blah, blah.)
OR
Jack: "Sure, but before I do, could you tell me a little more about the position itself?" (This is a flip.)

Jack flipped to get more detailed information before he addressed the question. A good salesperson will always want to get at a more detailed level of conversation.

A flip is a tool to watch for during the interview. Is the sales candidate just answering the buyer's questions, or is he probing at getting more detailed questions out? Flipping is a great sales tool, and one you need to be on the lookout for during the sales interview.

* *Three Levels of Why.* What do you like to do? Why? If you probe deep enough, you will find out the real reason. This is what we are looking for in a great salesperson. The ability to probe deep and question the motives of a buyer so that the real reason for a request or question can surface. The salesperson who can get to the real reason a buyer is ultimately asking his questions is a very good salesperson. We call this person one who has the ability to go to the Three Levels of Why (Figure 4-16).

If you were asked, "Why did you buy the watch you have on today?" you might answer with a rapport reason. If probed deeper, you would probably give a rationalization reason. If probed a little deeper, you would give a real reason. The real reason is the only place you can change someone's behavior.

Three Levels of Why Example

Q: *Why did you buy that watch?"*

A: "I liked it. It was attractive." (First level)

Q: *"I'm sure there were many attractive watches out there for you to choose from. Why that particular watch?"*

Figure 4-16. The Three Levels of Why.

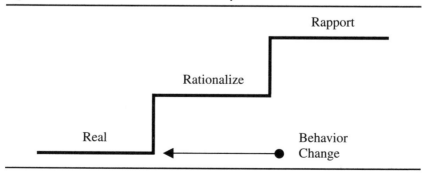

A: "It was attractive. I also thought it looked durable." (Second level)

Q: *"That's great. There are probably hundreds of watches out there that are attractive and durable. Why that particular watch?"*

A: *"OK,* I'll tell you why I bought this watch! It looked sporty and looked like the kind of watch I want to run with in the marathon next month. I wanted a watch that would help make me feel like a champion marathon runner!"

Three Levels of Why is a sales technique that allows salespeople to answer real issues the buyer has and avoid the rapport and rationalization reasons a buyer, or an interviewer, can think of.

Three Levels of Why—Interview Example

Q: *"Why is the sales position open?"*

A: "We are a growing company and are constantly looking for good people." (First level)

Q: *"I see. Would there be any other reasons for this territory to be open as opposed to somewhere else?"*

A: "We think this market is a good one and want to penetrate it." (Second level)

Q: *"That's wonderful. But what is it about this particular market that makes you want to invest more resources in it?"*

A: "Well, now that you ask, we think this territory has been underperforming for the last two years, and we think we can get a lot more out of it, especially in the major accounts."

The third-level answer is a far cry from, "We are a growing company," the manager's first-level answer. The candidate now knows more about the buyer's current needs and can specifically address the real reason, rather than the rationalization (second level) or the rapport (first level) reasons.

Three Levels of Why is a sales skill that good salespeople have. You need to be on the lookout for it during the interview. Watch for the sales candidate to probe and really question you on issues. Those who take you at face value the first level will be the ones who take a buyer at face value. The ones who go to Three Levels of Why—now there's someone with solid sales skills.

Getting to the real reason with a buyer is very important for a salesperson. Watch for the same characteristic in a sales interview.

Who Closes Whom

You want a salesperson who can close, who can ask for the order. Same characteristic we are looking for in an interview. At the end of the interview, who closes whom? Does the candidate summarize the meeting and propose a next step, or is he just happy to hear from you again?

Who Closes Whom Example

Example #1

Q: *"Well that's about it. Thanks for coming."*

A: "Thank you."

Example #2

Q: *"Well that's about it. Thanks for coming."*

A: "Thank you, Mr. Smith. One more thing. You said you would be done with the first round of interviews by the 15th. I will call you about that time to follow up with the next step, okay?"

The "buyer" closed Example #1. The candidate closed Example #2. Look for selling skills, even at the end of the interview. If the candidate closes the interview, he will close the sales call. Same thing.

These are the sales attributes on which to evaluate the sales candidates during the interview process. Many sales managers get caught up on past work history, dates of employment, and for whom someone has previously worked. These areas should be evaluated. However, you are looking for someone who can *sell*, so when all is said and done, treat the interview like a sales call, and evaluate it from that perspective.

Characteristics of a Great Salesperson

There are essentially five characteristics of great salespeople. They are:

- Natural Curiosity
- Complex to Simple
- Quiet Competence
- Ability to Flip
- All Three Perspectives

Natural Curiosity

Successful salespeople have a natural curiosity. They always want to know why. They take this inquisitiveness into the market and really know how to probe and ask good questions. They also tend to have good listening skills, which helps them ask great questions. Great salespeople do not always have the answers, but they always have great questions.

Complex to Simple

Successful salespeople can make the most complicated issue seem simple. At least they can explain it in simple terms. We call this putting it into third-grade language. A great salesperson would not make the following statement:

> "The complexity of this new product is evolving from our UL I program to our UL II program. It also comes with our GSM, GTT, GFR, and our new PPL modules, all designed to run at new gigahertz speeds."

The salesperson who made this claim knew exactly what she was talking about. The problem is she was the only one in the room who understood it. Keep things simple and explainable. Great salespeople avoid making themselves look good by impressing the buyer with their product knowledge. They communicate in simplistic terms and are understood because of it. For example, the salesperson could have said the following instead:

> "The advancement we now have in our new product will help you do the job twice as fast. Along with our additional modules, you will even be able to accomplish the task at least 10 times faster."

Quiet Competence

Great salespeople know they are great. They have a quiet competence about themselves. The other type, the insecure ones? They always talk about themselves. How great they are or how successful they are.

The good ones are confident in themselves and they will tell you how successful they are going to make you. They do not need a "job." They are A players. They can get a "job" anywhere. They are evaluating you and making sure the conversation is focused on you. They do this for two reasons. First, they are evaluating you and your company and want to find out as much as they can about you. Second, they know it makes the interviewer feel good to have them talk about themselves. It is true on a sales call, so it obviously works in an interview.

Ability to Flip

As discussed earlier, the ability to flip is an important one. Getting the buyer to talk is a characteristic of a successful salesperson. The person who flips in an interview has control of the interview or sales call. What is your opinion about this?

All Three Perspectives

The successful salesperson can see things from all perspectives. The great salespeople can hold a conversation from three different viewpoints when the situation calls for it. Watch for the candidate to switch from "I" to "You" to "They" mode when the situation calls for it. It is a thing of beauty.

The salesperson who can demonstrate all five sales competencies should be considered a top-notch candidate and worth further evaluation. Finally, remember the Golden Rule of Hiring sales candidates:

The Golden Rule of Hiring

Hire A players, period. It is easier to teach a competent salesperson what to sell than to teach a product-competent person how to sell.

ProActive Reference Checks

Finally, we will look at reference checks. There are five key things to remember about reference checks:

- Do them! It is absolutely amazing what you will learn from spending time doing a reference check about a candidate. You must do reference checks before an offer is extended.
- Have two sources do reference checks. In addition to the hiring manager, ask someone else, such as someone in human resources, the recruiter, or a peer. It creates a balance between the sales manager and another objective party. Too many managers have treated a reference check lightly, hearing only what they want to hear, not what really is being said. An outside party is more objective and can "hear" things a manager too close to the situation will not.
- Each person doing reference checks should do a minimum of two to three, for a total of four to six reference checks for each person you are about to hire. Use the reference check form shown in Figure 4-17 to write down responses and evaluate all checks that were completed by the other person, as well as the calls you had made. Many sales managers claim that reference checks are really not

Figure 4-17. How to conduct a reference check.

Steps to Conducting a Reference or Record Check

1. Introduce yourself.
2. State your purpose.
3. Apologize for interrupting the day.
4. Say how important it is for you to make a correct selection.
5. Ask permission to ask a few questions regarding the candidate.
6. If reluctant, or if referred to human resources, acknowledge your own reluctance to divulge information and your similar policy. Offer to go "off the record" (and mean it!) and appeal again for help in understanding the applicant's background and strengths.
7. State that you have knowledge of what the candidate's responsibilities were, but ask for an explanation of them, along with accomplishments (and possible failures) to get additional perspective.
8. Ask for strengths, assets, things liked and respected about the candidate, personally and professionally. Ask for more. When the list runs out, add any that you think are assets and have not yet been listed. (This person will begin to feel the candidate is getting full credit for all assets.) Obtain elaboration on strengths, so much so that the person with whom you are talking might become embarrassed at saying so many positive things about the candidate and may want to say a negative or two to make the assessment seem more balanced.
9. What were any shortcomings or possible areas for improvement? Don't interrupt—get the list of shortcomings, and only after this list has been exhausted entirely, go back to clarify and obtain specifics.
10. Describe the position and person specification (if it has not been done earlier in your conversation).
11. Put negative words in the person's mouth, in order to test your hypotheses about particular shortcomings. ("Would you say that punctuality was a problem?")
12. Ask the circumstances in which the person left. Was it 100 percent the person's own initiative, termination, or mutual? Would you rehire the person?
13. Close the conversation. Ask if there are any further comments. Ask if there are any other individuals who could provide additional information about the applicant. Thank the individual for being helpful, make reassurances regarding confidentiality (if promised), and say good-bye.

---

a good source of information about the candidate. A good candidate would only put down a reference that would give her a good reference, right? Others claim to have uncovered information from references the candidate provided to them that influenced their decision *not* to hire the candidate.

- If desired, reference checks to verify educational background or degrees can be obtained from schools. Have your human resources person help you out in this area.
- If someone will not give you a reference because of company policy, find out whether that is indeed the reason. It is quite common for a candidate to feel a coworker or boss will give him a great reference, when in actuality that person's view of the candidate is not favorable at all. Thus, when a reference provided by the candidate refuses to give you any information, you should start paying attention. When a candidate-supplied reference claims he is limited in divulging information, it is either because he is limited by his current company policy, or there is a hidden message. Time to find out what it is.

The Offer That Works

You are in the home stretch. Now is the time to be very clear on the steps you wish to take to secure the hire.

Professionalism and image are extremely important. This is the time the candidate's fear of change will start to surface. Your company image and professionalism will be the key to overcoming this fear. Identify expectations on both sides and gain agreement. "This is what you are looking for and this is what we are offering. Is this correct?" Ask that up front and in the offer letter.

Make the offer as soon as possible. Present the offer in person. If this is not possible, overnight mail is the next best choice. You are looking for the candidate's acceptance in writing. Set a time frame when the offer is due back, typically within 24 to 48 hours and, if at all possible, never give the candidate a weekend to think about it. The weekend allows the candidate to drift back into her comfort zone. This may lessen her desire to change. Fridays are always a great time to gain a commitment.

The Counteroffer

You must always believe that a counteroffer from the candidate's current employer is in the making. If you find a strong candidate, you are not the only one who thinks, *"This is a good one."* There are three things you can do to assist the candidate with the counteroffer.

First, use your homework. During the interview process you uncovered quite a lot about why the candidate is leaving. Highlight why the candidate is seeking other employment and why her current situation does not satisfy her needs. Remember, the #1 reason salespeople leave a job is the inability to learn and grow.

Second, prepare the candidate for her current employer's counteroffer. By doing that, you will have developed a comfort zone with her. If she knows to expect a counter, she will feel more comfortable dismissing it and will be less stressed about the change in employment.

Third, take it seriously. Is it more money? Is it a better position? Is it truly a better offer? Be objective. Stress that the counteroffer is being made because the candidate is filling a current management need. Is the real reason for the counteroffer being addressed? Will the offer really come to fruition? How you come across during this time is extremely important. Your objectivity and professionalism should carry through to assist the candidate to make the right decision.

When Not to Offer

There may come a point at the end of the evaluation where you are just not sure if you should go through with the interview process and present an offer letter to the candidate. Two blind spots may halt the offer process.

1. *Bad Reference Checks.* When the reference checks are not congruous with what has been stated during the interview process, it is obvious that something is amiss. You must go back and

reevaluate your interview process or your reference checks. Your decision is to either dismiss the candidate or present the candidate with the reference evaluations and discuss.

2. *Stalling*. The candidate may want to stall before accepting the offer or use this time to negotiate. Some of this negotiation should be allowed. It is a sales situation and both sides must win. If the stalling or negotiating is over the top, your gut will tell you that something is wrong. Be aware that this may be the sign to dismiss the candidate or force a decision.

The Subjective Interview: The Final Assessment

The final assessment of an interview should be based on your subjective feeling (gut reaction). It is very hard to dismiss with objectivity when the sales candidate has met all the decision criteria but subjectively your gut is telling you that something is wrong. When you get to this level make sure it is not personal bias. If it is, dismiss it.

But if it is indeed not the culture match you are looking for, your subjective evaluation could be causing your gut to start an alarm bell ringing. If this is the case, you must back away from the situation and evaluate.

The subjective part of the interview begins with your "gut feeling." Every employment interviewer leaves every interview with a gut feeling about the candidate. What is this gut feeling? Where does it come from? What should be done about it?

Gut feelings are positive or negative responses to very subtle messages sent and received on a nonverbal, subconscious level. The candidate, through tone or pitch of voice, eye and body movements, or general appearance factors, communicates the subliminal messages. These messages may be too subtle to be "noticed" consciously, but they are recorded and processed by the equally subtle senses of the brain's right hemisphere.

If the sum of these impressions is negative, it may be because the candidate is in some way triggering an unconscious prejudice in the interviewer. Most people have an image of acceptability more or less consciously defined. If the candidate is too far outside your range of acceptability, you will have a negative reaction, regardless of the candidate's qualifications. If your gut feeling is negative, check to see whether it is just caused by the appearance factor. If it is and it is merely a personal basis and will not affect job performance, discount it.

Another, more subtle source of negative gut feelings is your intuitive perception of a discrepancy between what the candidate's words say and what the reality is. When people speak the truth as they know it, their words and their nonverbal signs and signals are "congruous," creating a feeling of trust and confidence. The reaction is positive and you will "feel good" about that candidate.

If there is a discrepancy or conflict between what candidates say and what they know to be so, that discrepancy will be communicated to you in very subtle ways—through eye movements, tone of voice, body language. Those negative feelings that you "just can't put your finger on" are an alarm bell to which you should pay attention. Your right hemisphere is telling you that something about the candidate isn't right.

On the other hand, it is possible that the negative impression has been created by the candidate's response to the stress of the interview itself. This is why it is so important to have "de-stressed" the candidate as much as possible, not so that you can catch them off guard, but so that your "reading" of the subliminal message will be accurate. If a candidate seems unable to relax during the interview in spite of your genuine attempts to de-stress him, it indicates his low tolerance for stress or a strong probability of incongruity between words and reality.

Your gut feelings, whether positive or negative, should definitely be taken into account in your hiring decisions. They should not, however, be allowed to dominate the decision-making process. They can confirm or contradict your "rational" analysis for the candidate. Use both your objective and subjective evaluations to make your decision.

Celebrate Success: Closing the Deal

You have done your job. You have made the offer, the candidate has accepted, but you are not home yet. Make sure that both parties have written acceptance, and confirm the start date and the job description again, if possible in a face-to-face meeting at the company facility. Know when your candidate is going to resign from her current employer, for obvious reasons.

Now is the time for your candidate to feel accepted by the company. Walk her around and introduce her as a new employee. This is a good way to let her genuinely feel that she is welcome as a new team member. Show her where she will be working and have her sit in her new office. If she works from another location (e.g., a home office), have coworkers call the new employee to welcome her aboard.

If she works in the main office, have her business cards and/ or name tag ready on her first day of work. Have her office set up. Give her two measurable objectives for her first week, for example meeting three company vice presidents, or contacting the person who has been in the company the longest. This will give her exposure in the company. It will give her a mission—something for you to talk about at the end of the week. Have lunch with her sometime near the end of the first week to let her know you want to take time to make sure everything is going well.

These things may seem to be of little significance, but they are very important in conveying the right first impression to the new employee.

Make her feel accepted and share in the excitement that has been generated during the interview process. If possible, help her celebrate her success as well. Does your company allow $25 gift certificates, or are bottles of champagne accepted in your company culture? Start off on the right foot with the new hire as a successful member of your sales team.

Celebrate success! You have done a successful job, and now you can put your training, coaching, and counseling skills to work. The ProActive Sales Manager is always on the lookout for top sales candidates. With the interviewing and hiring skills just covered, you have increased your chances of getting top performers to join your team. The really good ones are hard to find, but armed with good interviewing and hiring skills, you now have the tools to know who you are looking for, to hire the right candidates, and to motivate them to achieve their goals.

Congratulations. You have increased your chances to hire the right salesperson the first time! Now go and start the process all over again.

Chapter 5

Corrective Action

Corrective action does not mean firing someone. If you need to fire someone, do it. If something has been done to cause immediate termination, then terminate. Going down a path of corrective action when the employee needs to be terminated is only going to delay the inevitable. It's important to keep in mind that if the day arrives when you need to terminate an employee, you must follow the legal and human resources policies and guidelines your company has defined. The legal guidelines vary by company, so check with your human resources department before terminating an employee.

Corrective action has a purpose. The objective of corrective action is to notify an employee when he needs to make an improvement, and give him an opportunity to improve. Indiscriminate firing of people is not corrective action. Corrective action is a process a manager should undertake only when she believes there is actually an opportunity for the employee to improve.

Starting a Corrective Action Process

There are only three main reasons to start a corrective action process.

- When ethics have been compromised, for example, when an employee is caught lying or stealing. In some extreme cases, immediate termination would be appropriate as opposed to a corrective action process.

- When performance over time has not been meeting expectations. Let's call this Gap Management.
- When the cost of retraining an employee is more expensive than rehiring. In business, bottom line results need to be respected.

Remember, the objective of corrective action is to notify the employee there is a behavior or an action that is unacceptable and needs attention. By going through a corrective action process, it is the desire of both the manager and the employee to improve the situation. This must be the goal of both parties.

The Corrective Action Process

Many sales managers are concerned about when to start the process of termination. There are a thousand and one reasons to delay, stall, wait, and drag one's feet—to take decisive corrective action later rather than sooner. For example:

"Maybe I should wait another quarter. Things aren't that bad."

"The devil you know. I'll just wait and see what happens."

"I know I should do something, but I will be short a person in the territory and finding good people is hard."

"Better him in the territory than no one."

"I'm really good at avoiding conflict."

How do we begin a corrective action process? This is probably one of the most difficult things a manager has to do. It's never easy to tell an employee he is not performing up to expectations. There are many emotions and opinions that surface during this time.

There is a tremendous amount of anxiety and fear on the employee's part, including fear of failure, fear of the unknown, and fear of poverty. There is also anxiety on the part of the manager. With such a wide range of emotions and fears circling around, a simple, straightforward process and methodology are required. The corrective action process consists of four sequential steps:

1. Counseling
2. Written Warning
3. Final Written Warning
4. Termination

By using this process, you are following a step-by-step process that allows the employee every chance to improve.

Counseling

It is important to approach the corrective action process in a counseling and empathetic manner. Usually, the employee knows there are problems, and her objectivity is clouded by emotions of inadequacy and fear. The manager should bring a sincere and employee-centric viewpoint to the discussion. A counseling session will allow the meeting between the manager and employee to get at the real issues and create an air of mutual trust. The following quotes illustrate the proper counseling approach:

> "John, your results have been off for a few weeks now . . . what's up?"

> "Jim, what's the deal with coming into the office late? It's been going on for a few weeks now and I am a bit concerned."

> "Mary, I have been informed that your colleagues find you very argumentative and difficult to get along with. What's going on?"

By approaching the first session in a counseling and empathetic manner, you will be able to set a tone of concern and openness, and one where the employee can discuss the situation freely without the negative emotions that surround the corrective action process.

The manager's attitude also needs to be addressed here. Many managers will try to distance themselves from the employee who is not doing well. They will ignore them, avoid them, and talk in a negative way about them to peers, bosses, and office administrators. In these situations the manager is looking for support for their uncomfortable decision. They need to vent and get other opinions to validate what they are doing.

This "getting the rest of the pack excited so the weakest dog can be thrown out" culture is not helpful. If you need to talk about a situation, talk with one peer or your boss. Once a decision is made, talk about what is going to happen when this employee is on a plan, not what they did to get on one. The more supportive the group, the better the chance of success for the employee.

This counseling session is an important first step. By specifically linking the problem to the desired results, you may be able to eliminate steps in the corrective action process. However, if more steps are needed since employee performance has not improved, the faster you go through the next steps, the better.

Written Warning

After a suitable amount of time, usually a few weeks, if the problem situation still exists, it is time to proceed past the counseling stage. A written warning is the next step used to formally notify the employee that there is a situation you and the company feel still needs to be corrected, since earlier counseling sessions have not brought about the desired change. By using a written document, you are:

- Formally informing the employee there is a situation that needs to be corrected.
- Starting a documentation trail that will be legally useful if you need to terminate the employee.
- Conveying the seriousness of the situation to the employee.
- Notifying management there is a situation that needs management attention.
- Paving the way for additional steps in the formal process.

Using a written warning should not been seen as a desperate measure or as a final step. It is a natural step in a corrective action process aimed at improving performance. This is similar to a doctor prescribing medicine so the patient will get well, not sicker. With a written warning, you are "prescribing" written information that tells the employee you want the situation to get better. It is a tool to be used with the attitude that things will get better, not worse.

A typical formal first warning is shown in Figure 5-1. How you write this letter and adapt it to your company policy and legal requirements is up to you. The text of the letter should state:

1. Your identification of a situation that needs correcting
2. Your desired action and remedy
3. A stated next step to be taken if the desired action is not corrected

It is not necessary to go into a flowery discussion about the problem, or how you intend to help the employee through this situation. While the employee is not legally required to sign the letter, it may be a good idea because it represents a show of commitment. Nor is it necessary to have a witness present.

Figure 5-1. Sample letter: first written warning.

Dear _____ :

It has come to the attention of myself and of the management of this company that you _____ (state reason for this written warning). This is not in line with our current expectations or company norms.

It is our desire to see your performance improve _____ (state desired improvement goals, measurable over a specified time frame).

We would like for you to achieve the above-stated level of performance. If this does not happen within the time frame stated, further disciplinary action may be taken up to and including termination.

Sales Manager

Again, use discretion and consult your company's policy on these matters. Most important is your documentation and your intent to follow through. Be as specific as possible to the salesperson regarding what action you want him to take. You need to use metrics to make sure that the employee understands where he is currently not performing to standards, and what specific performance is required to get back on track.

Metrics will work in cases of performance problems. In ethics infractions, theft, or physical violence, a statement of the behavior and demanding the behavior be stopped at once is appropriate. If the situation is bad enough, it may be cause for immediate termination. If you and the company decide there will be no immediate dismissal, then the appropriate action is a written warning or the establishment of some measurable objective over time.

The formal written warning is your first step in getting the employee back on track. To view it as anything else would be to expect failure, which is not the purpose of the corrective action process.

Use of Metrics

In the formal corrective action process, when performance is the issue at hand, you'll need a way to measure and chart improvement.

As you may recall from Chapter 1, metrics need to be mutually agreed-upon and measurable over time (M^2O/t). For the corrective action process, the mutually agreed-upon part need not be adhered to. But it is beneficial when the employee "owns" the corrective action being requested. Since this may not be possible in every case, try to gain agreement, but know that in the end, what counts is the performance improvement you believe is necessary.

What performance metrics should you measure to? The ones you are familiar with: Revenue, Frequency, and Competency metrics, of course.

Your letters must cover the revenue impact, if any, and what frequencies and/or competencies you expect to be accomplished over the next time period.

These R, F, and C measurements will allow both you and the employee to define a path to a positive outcome. If the employee chooses not to follow this path, you will have no choice but to notify her of her failure to live up to the objectives *she* agreed to, and that *her* action will cause you to take further action. By using corrective action in this manner, you place the ownership of the issue on the employee's back, not on yours. The written warning shown in Figure 5-2 illustrates the use of metrics.

It is not easy to start a corrective action process. You know this, your boss knows this, and so does the entire sales team. As a matter of fact, your indecision on taking ProActive corrective action measures can be viewed by the sales team as indecisiveness and lack of leadership on your part.

When you need to take corrective action, remember the corrective action rule:

If you are going to fail, *fail fast.*

This is not the time to put down this book and start corrective action on 30 percent of your people. You want to take an assessment of the situation and proceed accordingly. Use the S.O.S. Pyramid we discussed in Chapter 1 to formulate your plan of action. If you are in a situation where the desired results or a situation needs to be addressed, take action sooner than later. You'll be glad you did:

"I cannot believe I waited so long. What was I afraid of?"

"Everyone knew the situation. I was just rationalizing why I shouldn't take the first step."

"Performance improved drastically. He told me he was waiting for me to come to him and talk to him. Figure that one out!"

Fear of the unknown is powerful. We believe that if we say nothing or just prod a little, the situation will get better. But it rarely does. More important, it sends a powerful message to the sales team, to your manager, and to the rest of the organization of your inability to address a potential liability.

Figure 5-2. Sample letter: written warning using metrics.

Dear _____ ,

    Your performance over the past _____ months has not met the goals and objectives we agreed to at the beginning of the year.

    Specifically, your revenue is _____ percent below plan, and your new business is _____ percent below plan. This is not acceptable. You need to improve your performance and get back to our agreed-upon plan. Therefore, you need to accomplish the following tasks:

- Make twenty new sales calls per week to our agreed target list of accounts over the next sixty days.
- Take a sales training course to improve your sales skills. This must be accomplished in the next sixty days.
- Reach a target revenue of _____ percent at the end of this month, and _____ percent by the end of next month.
- Close one new business deal in excess of $_____ per week.
- Contact all thirty-five of your existing accounts over the next thirty days and develop five new qualified leads that we will both agree on in accordance with our qualified account guidelines.

    If any or all of the actions are not met, further disciplinary action may be taken, up to and including termination.

    It is my sincere desire to help you in obtaining these goals. The decision by you to work toward accomplishing these objectives is yours to make. We are here to assist you in any way feasible to ensure your continued success.

Sales Manager

    Fail fast means that if you are undecided, take action and do not wait. By being ProActive and addressing the potential problem, the upside is a more productive employee and a better sales team culture. By waiting, your indecision may cost you your job. The choice is clear. If you are in a correcting situation, be ProActive and get one step ahead of the problem. Start the first step, the counseling session, as soon as possible.

Final Written Warning

You have followed a process from a counseling session to a written warning stating what specifically you want the employee to do. When further action is required because the employee has not fulfilled the stated goals, a final written warning is needed. The final written warning is the same as the first written warning in that it:

- States specifically what the situation is that needs to be addressed.
- States the metrics needed to improve the situation.
- States the desired outcome.
- Informs the employee of further disciplinary action up to and including termination.
- States a specific time frame.

Figure 5-3 illustrates a final written warning. By taking this final step, you will be in a situation where definitive action is going to be taken, one way or another. If the employee turns

Figure 5-3. Sample letter: final written warning.

Dear _____ ,

On November 7, 2008, you were notified that your performance was not up to the sales team's and company's level of expectations as defined in your sales compensation and quota letter. This is unacceptable.

If the goals we discussed in our letter of November 7, 2008, are not met within the next _____ days, further disciplinary action may be taken, up to and including termination.

It is my desire to see you succeed. However, you must meet the outlined goals to continue your employment with the company. It is your responsibility to meet these goals, and I am willing to assist you in doing so.

Sales Manager

---

around, both parties win. If the employee moves on, both parties win.

Termination

Firing someone is not an easy task. There is no one right way to terminate an employee, and, as was previously stated, if the day arrives when you need to take that action, you must follow the legal and human resources policies and guidelines your company has defined. The guidelines vary by company, so check with your company to ensure you are legally compliant and are following your company's procedures on termination. We cannot offer specific legal recommendations, but we can offer some termination guidelines if the situation arises.

Termination Guidelines

1. *Never in Your Office.* Use a conference room, the employee's office, the human resources manager's office, anywhere but your office. Why? Because you can't leave. If the employee wants to stay and talk, and you don't, you are literally and physically trapped. Not a good situation to be in.

2. *Same Breath.* With the same breath with which you walk in the door you say, "The reason I am here right now is to inform you that this is your last day of employment with this company." Just get it out. Make it final. It makes the rest of the conversation more productive for both parties. No hemming and hawing. Spending 10 to 20 minutes setting the stage for you to discuss the situation leading up to termination is a waste of time for everyone involved.

3. *Don't Take a Chance.* The employment situation is based on a relationship. You never can fully understand the other party's intentions in this relationship. Don't take chances; you never know if the other party is going to overreact with physical abuse—whether it's toward yourself, himself, or even to office property.

4. *Fail . . . Fail Fast.* Self-explanatory. Take action Pro-Actively. Sooner rather than later.

5. *Never on a Friday.* If at all possible, try not to terminate on a Friday. For two reasons:

One, the employee has no opportunity to take action and start the process of feeling good about himself. All he can do is stew about it over the weekend. If terminated on, say, a Wednesday, the employee can call a few friends, recruiters, and business acquaintances and get things moving in a positive direction. This is good for the employee, as well as for you.

Two, the employee has nothing to do all weekend but associate the firing with you. You are the last official message from the company that fired him, and to be directly linked with these feelings is not a good thing. Give the employee more time to take some positive action rather than letting him brood about it over the weekend with thoughts of you. Never on a Friday, unless it is absolutely necessary.

6. *Over Your Head.* If the employee starts to bring up that he has consulted an attorney, stop the conversation immediately and turn the situation over to human resources or in-house counsel. If neither is available, stop the conversation and dismiss the employee immediately. You are not versed in the legal issues of terminations, and all you can do here is lose. Stopping the conversation immediately is a wise course of action.

7. *No Hanging Around.* Having the terminated employee hang around to clean out his office or finish up the day is a bad idea. End the relationship immediately. Personal effects can be retrieved from the desk in a few minutes, but then have the employee leave the premises. If he needs to come back, have him do so before or after hours when security or a manager is present. This is different if an employee quits, and you want him to hang around for a day or longer. In a termination, get him out as soon as possible.

8. *One Right Way.* Over the phone or in person? What is the right way to terminate an employee? There is no one right way. If you fly the employee in or you travel to his place, he will ask why you incurred the cost and time of travel. If you terminate over the phone, he will say you are too impersonal. Use your

best judgment. Over the phone, in person, whatever is right for the situation. Do an S.O.S. if you have to think about it. Use the most time-effective and situation-effective choice.

The previous guidelines and tips are to be used in a termination. You must obviously take termination seriously. The following story provides a good illustration.

A situation arose many years ago where an employee had to be terminated. He had been caught stealing from the company and lying to cover it up. When the facts were revealed, the sales manager and his boss decided to terminate the employee immediately. Because the employee worked in a satellite office in another city, the manager was going to fly in midmorning, terminate the employee, and return late in the afternoon. He felt it would be best if he went in person.

On the morning of his scheduled trip, he received a phone call from one of the other salespeople in the remote office. The conversation went something like this:

"Bill, are you coming down here to fire Mike today?"
"Gail, I cannot get into that."
"Bill, I have to know."
"Why?"
"Because Mike and I were talking this morning and he believes you are coming here to fire him today. He is not happy about it. In fact, he mentioned there are a few things you do not know about him. For instance, in Desert Storm, he was a commando. His job was to hide behind enemy lines during the day and go on seek-and-destroy missions at night. He's a trained killer! As a matter of fact, I am calling you from home, because I am afraid of what he might do to me or my family if he knew I was calling you."

Bill called his boss immediately. After a lengthy discussion with his boss, human resources executives, and the company lawyer, they *all* determined it was safe for *him* to go and fire Mike. The support team did give him a few pointers:

- Go to a public place—a restaurant, a coffee shop, somewhere where there is a crowd.

- If you feel insecure, rent a security officer. This will be money well spent.

- Forget about company assets right now. You can get them later. Going to the employee's house to gather computers or other capital equipment should be of secondary concern.

- If Mike has a company car, and you are in a situation where you believe it will not be an amicable meeting, have him turn in his car and offer him taxi fare for his ride home. The best alternative is to have the leasing company take care of this detail as well.

- The shorter the meeting, the better.

Armed with this information, Bill flew in and completed the termination meeting to perfection. Well, not exactly.

Fast forward to Bill and Mike sitting in a conference room with no windows and the door closed. Twenty minutes into the conversation, Bill is still hemming and hawing about a lot of issues except the one he is there for.

Finally, after 20 minutes or so, Mike asks, "Bill, are you here to fire me?" Mike gulped and struggled to say yes.

"OK, would you like me to leave now or at the end of the day?" Mike asked.

"Now would be fine," Bill replied.

The story had a happy ending. It was executed all wrong. The manager got lucky. Follow the guidelines. They will help.

It's Not Your Responsibility

It is always good to change one's perspective in the corrective action process. Remember, the employee has a problem, not you. It's their behavior that is causing you to take action. As a matter of fact, it is the employee not living up to the agreement she made with you that is causing further action. The employee is the one with the issue. If you have done a good job with your M^2O/t's, you will have:

- Mutually defined the situation with the employee.
- Stated the desired outcome in terms of objectives.

- Mutually agreed to the objectives.
- Given the objectives a time element.

The employee has made an agreement with you. If the performance or the correcting situation does not improve, it is because the *employee* is breaking the agreement with you. You cannot help her correct the problem situation. She needs to do that. It is what she agreed to. There isn't anything you can do to help her live up to the agreement. It is up to her. If further disciplinary action is required, it is because she made that choice.

Here are some final thoughts on corrective action and who is responsible:

- *Problem Solve.* Approach the issue as a chance to solve a problem. There is a behavior that needs correcting. Punitive action will yield only a short-term change in behavior. Approach the matter as one where both parties try to uncover the behavior that needs correcting.

- *Win-Win.* There must be a win-win course of action. Again, threats and punishments will make the employee change behavior in the short term, but in the end, these short-term punitive actions will cause the employee to get angry, get by, or get even.

- *Metrics—M²O/t.* Have both parties agree on the action that needs to happen for the behavior to change. And be sure to document everything.

- *Who Is Responsible.* The employee is the one who is breaking the agreement with you. She must take responsibility for her actions.

- *Decision-Making Day.* A final step before final termination proceedings should be a decision-making day. Meet with the employee early in the morning and explain that her behavior or actions are still unacceptable. Instruct her you are giving her the rest of the day off to go home and think about the situation. The next day, she will have a decision to make. Does she still want to work for you and the company? If yes, the M²O/t's need to be written down and agreed to. If not, the final termination proceedings will be initiated. Again, either way, the choice is the employee's. By giving her a day off with pay, she will know how serious the situation is. The choice is in her hands.

Coaching and Counseling Through the Process

The goal of corrective action is to inform the employee that there is a situation that needs correcting, and to give the employee an opportunity to improve. Through the use of effective coaching and counseling, which we discuss in the next chapter, you, the manager, can effectively stay on top of a situation and get it moving in the right direction.

Don't dread taking corrective action. Instead, think of yourself as an investigative reporter on an assignment. Your job is to uncover what is causing the situation and to report on it. It is also like being a doctor: Your job is to diagnose the problem and offer a prescription to fix it. Being a ProActive Manager means always being one step ahead, seeking out situations that may cause failure, and getting them corrected and back on the right track before they become issues. It is easy to stereotype and label people. This person is a "C" player or this person will "never amount to much." ProActive Managers stay one step ahead by using the tools we have provided. Your survival as well as your success depends on it.

Final Thoughts

It's been my experience that managers often wait too long to begin corrective action. Yet, it is what employees crave. Feedback on what to do correctly is a mainstay of management coaching. The lack of metrics and follow-up on the manager's part has caused many failures in the sales ranks.

Managers who use metrics properly, who communicate openly, and who catch people doing things right (as well as doing things wrong) should feel comfortable that they are ProActive.

Chapter 6

ProActive Management Skills

Coaching and Counseling: How to Be a Master Communicator in Any Organization

Great leaders are great communicators. How you communicate up, down, and sideways through an organization will determine in large part your success as a manager. There are a multitude of vehicles you can use to communicate effectively to the rest of the organization outside of the sales team.

Through memos, meetings, committees, quorums, e-mails, voice mails, and a host of other communication tools, you have many options to communicate effectively, beyond the sales team and throughout the organization.

To master the art of communicating down, we must add effective coaching and counseling to our sales manager's toolbox.

Coaching and Counseling

Let's define coaching and counseling. In our sales management classes, we typically would see *coaching* described in the following terms:

Telling	Directing	Instructing
Guiding	Leading	Doing

Listening	Providing Examples	Participating
Demanding	Maintaining Order	Prescribing
Teaching	Educating	Training

And *counseling* would be described in these terms:

Discussing	Consulting	Deliberating
Listening	Being Empathetic	Telling
Nudging	Advising	Leading
Prescribing	Agreeing with	Expressing Feelings

Judging from the words used to describe them, these two tools, coaching and counseling, are starting to look like they could be interchangeable. However, there is a big difference between them; and we need to understand that difference if we are to use these communication tools on a ProActive basis.

Coaching comes from our *interpretation of facts*. Managers coach from their own experiences, or from what they "know to be so" based on logic. Coaching sales calls involve the sales manager going out with a salesperson and assisting that person based on observations of the call itself (facts to the manager), or based on what the sales manager has learned from previous similar situations. Coaching is fact-based.

Counseling comes from your emotional side. Counseling is *personal and empathetic*. It is a powerful tool when you are looking for understanding and consensus. It is a tool to use when you want to elicit responses from the employee and arrive at a mutual arrangement. Counseling is empathy-based.

With these definitions, how is a sales manager to know which tool to use at which time? Wouldn't it be silly for the following scenarios to be played out?

Fourth down, and the football is on the five-yard line. Two seconds to go in the game. One play left. You need a touchdown to win. Pressure situation. The coach calls time out. He knows what to do. The quarterback comes running over to the sideline, turns quickly to the coach, and asks him what he should do, what can he do, to win the game. The coach knows. He looks the quarterback right in the eye and says to him:

"So, how are you feeling? Is everything OK? Every-thing OK at home? Anything I can do for you?"

Wouldn't this be a silly conversation?
Or take a workplace situation.

Suppose you have heard rumors that an employee may have a substance abuse problem. This makes you concerned. You like this employee a lot. He also happens to be a star performer. You have never had a problem with him before. Because you want to be Pro-Active, you call the employee into your office, shut the door, and very empathetically proclaim:

"I hear you may have a substance abuse problem. Fix it by tomorrow. Now go sell!"

Just as silly.

Let's use the right tool at the right time for the right situation. Welcome to the Coaching/Counseling Wheel.

The Coaching/Counseling Wheel

The idea of the wheel lines up with our idea of giving the sales manager tools for her toolbox. We want to use the right tool for the right situation. Let's explore all the tools.

In a coaching or counseling situation, you need to make sure that you use all the communications tools you have available. There are four dimensions to coaching and counseling:

- Positive Coaching
- Negative Coaching
- Positive Counseling
- Negative Counseling

You can use all four tools, but make sure you use the one that fits the right situation at the right time. All too often the sales manager will approach a situation with a tool she feels comfortable using. But is it the right tool for the right situation? The coaching/counseling wheel helps you to plan beforehand not only what to say, but *how best to deliver the message so the employee will hear it and understand it.* By using the four quadrants of the wheel, the content and the tone of the message will be ProActive. An example of each quadrant is illustrated in Figure 6-1.

There are four tools to help you deliver your message effectively. You may not be comfortable with one or more of them. That is not important. What is important is that you use the style you believe *will be most effective with the employee at the given time*, not the style with which you are most comfortable. Your job is to be effective with all communication skills, and to use the right one at the right time for your message to be heard and understood.

If you use the wheel during the S.O.S., you will deliver your objectives with the communication intent you desire. Develop your Situational analysis, establish your Objectives (determine which communication style will be the most effective), and then implement your Strategy. It fits right in to the process of managing with objectives and metrics, as we discussed in Chapter 1.

The Coaching Sales Call

While we are on the subject of coaching and counseling, let's discuss the coaching sales call. But first, let's consider a question that all sales managers ask themselves from time to time: "When is it OK to take over a sales call?"

There are many schools of thought on taking over sales calls. Should you save the sale and take over the call? Leave the salesperson on his own and let the call go the way he has planned it? Nudge? Hint? Just take it over and let the salesperson get his hands-on experience another time? What is a sales manager to do?

When the sales manager is on a sales call, a strange phenomenon happens. During the call, the sales manager is trying

Figure 6-1. Coaching and counseling wheel examples.

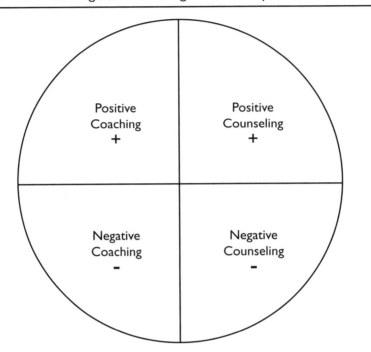

Examples of +/– coaching and counseling:

Positive coaching—"John, I have confidence in you that you can do this. I have seen you do this before, so go out there, call Ms. Smith, and get that order today!"

Negative coaching—"John, you have delayed long enough. If you do not call Ms. Smith today, further action will have to be taken by me, which may include you losing this account. Now go make that call."

Positive counseling—"John, I'm concerned about your call ratios. You must be as well. You have always been a top performer. What's up?"

Negative counseling—"John, I am very frustrated. This situation is very hard to understand. I do not know if there even is a solution. What is the problem?"

hard to let the salesperson control the call. Within a few minutes, the salesperson says something that the sales manager knows should be emphasized, elaborated, or expanded upon, but the manager says nothing. A few minutes later, same thing. The manager remains silent. When it happens a third time, the sales manager feels compelled to say something. Adding value is the rationalization. After 30 minutes, the sales manager is an integral part of the call. In some circumstances, the sales manager can even become the salesperson, taking over the call and rationalizing:

- It was necessary to save the call.
- It was a learning experience for the salesperson.
- It was too important for a coaching call.
- The salesperson learns by watching the pro.
- The sales manager gets paid for closing the sale, not to worry about who says what in a sales call.

The list of rationalizations could be endless, and each one perfectly valid.

What is a good coaching call and what are the rules and guidelines? To answer this question, we must look at three types of calls.

- The Coaching Call
- The Joint Sales Call
- The Unexpected Call

It is critical to determine which type of call you are making *before* the call itself. There are many reasons for this, but the obvious one is to allow each participant to know what role he should be playing. A successful sales call is strategized ahead of tine, and the outcome is planned, not the result of a fortunate turn of events. With the planning of a sales call as a prerequisite, it's time to look at all three types of sales calls.

The Coaching Call

In the coaching call, the salesperson has complete control. It could be a new prospecting call, a call to a current client, or a sales call early in the sales cycle. It should not be one where there is a lot to lose. The value of the call should be low to allow for mistakes and for the creation of a learning environment where the sales manager does not feel compelled to jump in. "Adding value" during the sales call should be avoided at all costs. If there is a need to jump in, it should be done tactfully through the salesperson, as shown in the following examples:

> "Kyle, I think I heard Mr. Lynch say he had a concern about the warranty term of the product."

> "Brad, I believe Mr. Bush wants to know the delivery terms for our product."

> "Betsy, do you think this is a good time to bring up the proposal we have been discussing with Mr. Zahka's people?"

A good coaching call is one where the sales manager allows the salesperson the freedom to succeed or fail. Any problems can then be discussed after the call is over. A good sales manager will rehearse the call with the salesperson beforehand, minimizing the need to jump in. If continual sales manager interruptions happen during the sales call, it means one of two things:

- The sales call was not planned out effectively, which means more planning is necessary before the next call.

- The sales manager has a propensity to jump in on sales calls and should learn to stay quiet.

The unofficial rule in a friend of mine's Little League baseball games is to have a good time, and when your child is up to bat, offer encouragement, but no coaching.

"Coaching," says my friend, "should be reserved for the front yard, not the ball field."

Managers need to manage, and they need to let salespeople sell. If you want to sell, go sell. If you want to manage, then make a plan and implement it.

A Coaching Sales Call Scorecard should be used on these calls (for one thing, it keeps the sales manager busy, productive, and out of the way). A Scorecard will allow the manager to keep track of the call and actually do some coaching, rather than merely making a subjective assessment after the call.

A good scorecard defines the mission and describes the coaching goals along the way.

The sales manager should develop a Scorecard for each call and review it with the salesperson before the call. In a true coaching call, the manager's job is to . . . coach! Have a game plan and coach to selling skills, not just to product knowledge and the ability to answer questions.

Another idea is to videotape the call. Using web collaboration software such as Cisco/WebEx, you can record the conversation and the video and review it later. Bring a video camera on a sales call and ask if you can use it. On a prospecting call, this probably will not go over too well. But if you describe the purpose of the call to a good long-standing customer, and you explain how it will benefit them, they probably will let you videotape the sales call.

You can think of a lot of ways to coach by watching sport coaches. They have clipboards, they watch game film, and they practice, practice, practice. When was the last time you had a practice session? Role-playing is great—once a month, and for no longer than 30 minutes.

The Joint Sales Call

As implied in the name, in a joint sales call, the sales manager plays an active role. When a sales situation is at a critical phase and needs management expertise, the salesperson may feel that the sales manager would enhance the process. In that case the sales manager is providing a planned value to the call itself.

Another good reason for a joint call is because the salesperson is new. The person can be new to the company, to the territory, or even new to sales. The sales manager in this joint call will have a larger than usual role to play. It is still the goal of a joint sales call to give salespeople a chance to stretch themselves. Before the call, determine what roles need to be played, and stick with the plan as much as possible. You may decide to have the salesperson open the call, have you handle the middle of the call, and have the salesperson close and propose a next step. Whatever the strategy, the roles should be determined before the call. This will make sure the call goes according to plan, and that the new salesperson won't be asked just to "watch and learn from the pro." People learn more by doing than by observing.

A successful joint sales call is like a play. The roles are carried out according to a prearranged script. However, many sales calls do not go according to the script, and you need to exercise good judgment on when it is acceptable to deviate from the script. How will the salesperson learn how to handle a sales call that goes a little awry if the sales manager is always there to save the day? The joint sales call is one where both parties plan to add value, not to take over each other's role.

The Unexpected Sales Call

Many sales calls fall into this category, such as uninvited guests from the prospect's side, a change of strategy midstream based on new information just uncovered during the call, or a critical timing change by the prospect that causes a new course of action. What should you do during such a call? You should use your best judgment.

If at all possible, your first option should be to let the salesperson try to figure it out. Salespeople will always have to deal with unexpected sales call situations. How well they handle them will depend on what they learn from handling such calls on their own.

A second option is to call for a short pause in the meeting for a side conference between you and your salesperson to readjust your strategy. Use your best judgment and try to work through, not around, the salesperson. Worst case, put the call back on track and have a coaching session after the call.

The unexpected call is the one where a good salesperson, along with the sales manager observing the situation, can become a great salesperson. It can only happen if the astute sales manager, working with the salesperson, works the sales call to this end. The great managers do.

Focus on the A Players

A final note on coaching sales calls: Make sure you are spending 70+ percent of your time on your A players or soon-to-be A players (new hires, Bs making strides to become As, etc.). You can go on all the C player coaching calls you want, but you will be:

- Helping your C players (fish!)
- Providing little ProActive help to your A players
- Losing an insurance policy—Show Me the Money

ProActively find the time to coach your As. By leaving them alone, you are turning into a neutral boss and creating a culture for B and C players. Make your culture an A culture and press your As to become A+ players. You can only do that by finding time to spend with them. Focus your coaching on your A players. The rest will come up to speed.

Coaching and Counseling
Your Boss Effectively

So how does one use these coaching and counseling skills to effectively communicate upward in the organization? Much has been written on the subject of working with the boss. Many books tell you how to manage upward; communicate upward; listen upward; how to talk to, with, and through the boss; and even how to ignore the boss. There is quite a bit of opinion on the subject. What we really want to add to the process is a set of metrics that facilitate communication with the boss, specifically, M^2O/t and $R = F \times C$.

Mutually agreed-upon measurable objectives over time tend to work just as well upward as downward in the organization. If you add in the $R = F \times C$ initiative, you come up with a set of tools that allows sales managers at all levels to communicate with their boss in a measurable and ProActive manner. This is accomplished in three ways.

1. *Understanding the Boss's Perspective.* Bosses are bosses for many reasons. One is that they see things from different perspectives. They have broader responsibilities and have to see things differently from their subordinates. Many managers believe passionately that they have the right answer or that they have the one right way of doing things. They also believe that not getting the boss involved is acceptable, since all the boss can really do is mess things up.

This is not a good strategy. The boss is the boss. She must be involved and she must be kept involved. In a sales situation, we might ignore the senior buyer, not ask the right questions because we're afraid of the answer we'll get. And we may be inclined to use the same strategy with the boss. But it won't work, so be ProActive and understand the boss's perspective. Get the boss on your team.

A great way to do this is the quarterly planning session. Most sales managers review the forecast with their manager, and believe this constitutes a great quarterly review. Here is an agenda you may want to copy for your quarterly reviews:

I.   Cover goals of the last quarter.
II. Cover goals of the coming quarter.
III. Gain agreement on goals from the boss and get their goals for the upcoming quarter.

This is to be done before the quarterly meeting in a memo, e-mail, or face-to-face meeting. There's nothing like gaining agreement on the meeting *before* the meeting. Then, the quarterly meeting agenda can look like this:

I.   Cover last quarter and this quarter goals from the boss's perspective.
II. Cover last quarter results and current quarter goals.
III. Forecast review.
IV. Action steps—M^2O/t and $R = F \times C$ to be used.
V.   Follow-up documentation.

2. *Formal Communication.* We must keep the boss formally informed on a ProActive basis, and to do this we need standards.

With M^2O/t and $R = F \times C$, we can be ProActive and gain the boss's agreement up front, and then keep the boss informed. No boss likes surprises, and if we understand this and use these tools to standardize our communication platform for the senior manager, we will lessen the senior manager's risk.

Risk is the most critical item a senior manager has to deal with. When risk is high, senior managers have a natural tendency to try to manage things themselves. Time and time again, when senior managers are heavily involved in the details of the organization, it is because they believe the risk of the situation is too great to stay out of it. They end up doing their subordinates' job because of this perceived risk. By increasing the formal communication to senior management, you reduce risk. By reducing risk, or increasing the confidence the boss has in you, you receive more freedom. Once again, by increasing formal communication to the boss, you lessen his risk, thereby increasing his ability to do the job the way he needs to do it.

What are the biggest risks your boss faces over the next three to six months? By knowing this, you can keep your sales team aligned not only to your goals, but to the company goals as well.

3. *Informal Communication.* Add informal communication to this equation, and we successfully manage upward. Three things that are important in this type of communication are:

- *Keep it positive.* Even in the wake of bad news, try to put things in a positive perspective.
- *Solutions.* Solutions are important. Anyone can identify problems. Helping to identify solutions and implementing them is the real issue.
- *Through their eyes.* Keep in mind the boss is the boss. Try to keep the conversation focused on what's important to him. After all, he is the boss.

Keeping him informed by using metrics and successful communication is an effective way to "manage" the boss.

As we discussed in an earlier chapter, there are three types of bosses: those who help, those who hurt, and those who are neutral. If you have a helping or neutral boss, these strategies will work. In a situation where you are not getting along with your boss, you have two choices:

- *Try to implement the previous strategies.* You may not have really understood the boss's situation.

Or

- *Fix the situation.* Come up with a mutual solution that may include you leaving. It may not be working out, and the sooner you and the boss identify this, the better off you will be.

Motivation—Know Why People Do What They Do and Be One Step Ahead

Why is motivation such a hot topic? One would think sales-people are charged up and fired up on a daily basis and motivating a sales team would amount to overkill. How do you motivate a sales team? Do the following quotes sound familiar?

"I need to learn how to motivate my sales team to keep them fired up every day."

"How can I motivate my salespeople to take the next step? To get them to work harder and have the same drive I did when I was a salesperson?"

"My salespeople need a good dose of motivation. How can I motivate them to go beyond the day-to-day stuff and really excel?"

These are requests from sales managers about their sales-people. There are some issues to deal with here. Before we do, let's take a look at what motivation is.

Many managers believe motivation is the ability to initiate, drive, cajole, require, master, coach, counsel, inform, mediate, administrate, or make others do something. What is it really? Motivation is a drive. It is a drive from the inner self. You cannot motivate anyone to do anything. Everyone is in charge of his or her own motivations. You can choose to allow external factors (emotions, actions, or events) to motivate you to feel, do, or think. You must choose to be motivated. Let's look at some motivational theory to better understand the concept.

According to the psychologist Abraham Maslow's Hierarchy of Needs, our needs progress from the most basic physiological level to higher-order needs, such as esteem and self-actualization (Figure 6-2). The five levels are:

Level 1—Basic Physiological Needs
Level 2—Safety and Security Needs
Level 3—Belonging and Social Needs
Level 4—Esteem and Status Needs
Level 5—Self-Actualization

We all start at the bottom—at the basic physiological needs like eating and sleeping. Once these needs are met, we move up

Figure 6-2. Maslow's Hierarchy of Needs.

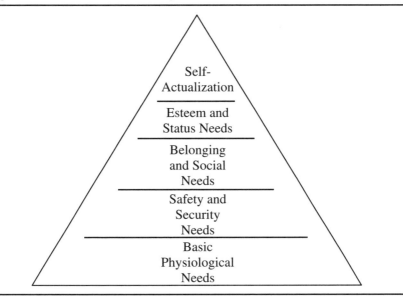

a level to safety and security needs, such as shelter and self-protection. Then we continue to move up, first to belonging and social needs (love, friends, family), then to esteem and status (the right friends, the right schools and clubs), and finally to self-actualization. Fredrick Herzberg took Maslow's model and divided it up into Maintenance Factors and Motivational Factors.

If we compare Maslow's and Herzberg's models, as shown in Figure 6-3, we find that according to Herzberg, the basic workplace factors are maintenance factors, such as peer relationships, basic working conditions, and pay. The motivational factors are the ones centered around:

- Praise
- Reward and Recognition
- Learn-and-Grow—Challenges

Figure 6-3. Comparison of Maslow's and Herzberg's models.

Hierarchy of Needs

Maslow	Herzberg	
Self-Actualization Esteem and Status Needs Belonging and Social Needs	• Work Itself • Achievement • Possibility of Growth • Responsibility • Recognition	Motivational Factors
Safety and Security Needs Basic Physiological Needs	• Peer Relations • Quality of Supervision • Job Security • Working Conditions • Pay	Maintenance Factors

If we want to understand why people do what they do, we need to look no further than these three motivational factors.

Praise

The old saying that you will attract more flies with honey than with vinegar is still true today. In fact, a little bit of kindness goes a long way. Successful salespeople are a rare breed. Their basic motivation is to make sure they are doing a good job for themselves and for others. That's why offering a salesperson heartfelt praise for an effective presentation, a job well done, or a successful sale is a powerful motivational tool. Some sales-people fear they may not be as good as they seem. They fear that they will start losing, and the fear of failure is a powerful motivator.

Sincere praise is an inexpensive but powerful motivator. Remember the 3 to 1 rule: Sales managers feel that they offer praise three times for every constructive criticism. But salespeople will tell you their boss offers three constructive criticisms for every word of praise! The 3 to 1 rule tells you to try to catch your salespeople doing something right three times as often as you criticize them for something wrong. What ProActive things have you done lately to catch some of your best salespeople doing something right?

Reward and Recognition

Reward and recognition, though similar to praise, are a bit more formal and can be ProActively targeted to situations that need attention. Rewards are a planned device to tell the sales team formally that they are doing something right. Rewards should be based on their having accomplished something that you wanted them to do, and they should not be just revenue based. Rewards should be measurable (M^2O/t) and focused on Revenue, Frequencies, and Competencies ($R = F \times C$). Some suggested rewards are:

- A reward for making the most sales calls in person to vice presidents and above over a 30-day time period.

- A reward for the most sales at list price over a 60-day period.
- A weekly award for the best win-win negotiation session.
- Monthly merit badge or similar token-award ceremonies, with letterman jackets, sweaters, or plaques.
- Monthly awards for the most qualified prospects in the A sales funnel.
- For telemarketing sales, a weekly award for the most attempts made or the most contacts actually made.
- The Magic Wand Award for the best deal of the week.
- Weekly notes on individual sales team stationery. Surely, your sales team has its own logo and team stationery to announce important new events and new customers.
- Monthly stack-ranking charts to identify who is leading and trailing the pack.

These ideas and similar ones can formalize the reward and recognition process. Make sure you put some excitement and effort behind these programs. Put your ownership behind the programs you implement.

Here are some rules about rewards:

- It is never the size or dollar amount of the award that is of primary importance; it is the amount of emphasis you put behind the reward that counts.
- Rewards should be short in duration, lasting no more than three to six months because the newness wears off, they become forgotten, and essentially they lose their effectiveness. Some monthly rewards can last for a year or two. As a general rule, the shorter the reward is in duration, the more focus it will get.
- Recognition needs to be positive. Negative recognition is a demotivator and should not be used. Naming someone ''Loser of the Month'' or the ''Person Who Still Does Not Have a Deal Yet'' creates a negative sales culture. Management may feel comfortable with it, but the salespeople will not learn and grow in such a culture.
- Rewards, like contests, should be singular in focus. Having multiple rewards at the same time lessens the impact

of the rewards. (I know of one company that gave a reward to every salesperson every month, regardless of the salesperson's performance. The company wanted to create a positive work environment. The salespeople got the reward every month, but since they had no idea why they were getting the reward, they made no additional efforts to obtain the rewards. The company has since changed this program to one that is metric-based, and it started measuring the results.)

- Any reward program should be fun. Make it fun for the salespeople. Get them involved in planning and executing contests. Too many managers have fun "anointing" contest winners, while the contest winner stands around smiling and not feeling involved.

One sales manager had a contest where she brought in a pair of extra large dice. Every week for three months she had the "Roll for Dough" contest. Every Friday, the salespeople would get together and each person who had closed a deal during the week got a chance to roll for dough. The number of deals during the week determined the number of rolls. The salesperson received $5.00 a point for each roll of the dice. Well, after a few weeks, this was just too much fun. People started dressing in Las Vegas dealer outfits. Armbands and dealer hats were used. Every Friday afternoon, you would hear this screaming from the sales department, "Come on, baby," or "Just blow on 'em, Hank." It was a major success and salespeople did not want to be left out of rolling the dice, so everyone worked really hard during the week to close more deals. The contest did not cost a lot of money, everyone had fun, and the reward program achieved its goals!

Learn-and-Grow Challenges

Top salespeople want to learn and grow. For some, it is the #1 motivational factor. The consistent development and application of these learn-and-grow challenges is a challenge in itself. How do we keep A players motivated in a learn-and-grow situation? After all, they still need to produce revenues. We want to keep the top salespeople focused on bringing in revenue and adding value, but we also need to come up with some creative ideas that will help them to push themselves and the rest of the sales team. How can this be done? Here are a few pointers:

- Assist in launching a new product.
- Take on the responsibility to make sure the next trade show develops *good* sales leads.
- Work with a rookie salesperson. Make internal presentations that you would normally make.
- Evaluate and implement a sales force automation tool you are considering.

The list goes on. The learn-and-grow factor is important.

- Have the A players come up with some additional ideas. Listen and try to accept them as good ideas before you dismiss them. We all have a natural tendency to reflexively dismiss or reject most new ideas.
- M^2O/t. You and the salespeople should discuss and agree on a learn-and-grow plan in addition to their current quota plan. A players know they need to make the numbers, as well as carry out added responsibilities. They will find a way to do both. That's what makes them A players. You will be surprised how much "free" time an A player can find if properly motivated.
- Training is an effective tool. Top salespeople and top sales managers want management to invest in their careers. Training is a win-win for the employee and the employer. More on this topic in Chapter 9.
- Ask other managers. Other departments in the organization have A players as well. They have to come up with ideas to motivate their top performers. It may be the finance department or engineering, but you can "steal" a good idea from many different organizations in your company and then adapt it to the sales team.
- Positive motivations centered around praise, rewards, and learn-and-grow challenges are a key element in hiring, motivating, and keeping top performers. They are a

major part of your sales team culture. What are you doing on a ProActive basis to keep your sales team motivated?

A note on motivating salespeople: Try to avoid "dumping" projects on a top performer. She may not share your goals. She may not want to participate in a program that makes *you* look good if there is nothing in it for her except extra work. Keep dumping to a minimum.

Motivational Direction

Motivational direction embraces the theory that a person is motivated either by pain or pleasure. Avoiding pain or seeking pleasure is the start of one's motivational direction. We can simplify this by assigning labels to people as being either pleasure-seeking types, or *toward* motivators, or pain-avoiding types, or *away* motivators. This identifies most people then as having a motivational direction of either *toward* or *away*.

Based on this classification, we want to motivate people according to how they want to be motivated, or in the direction in which they want to be motivated, either toward or away. Toward people sees things in a positive manner. If asked why they would buy a new pair of shoes, a new couch, or a new TV, they would respond in a *toward* manner, such as:

"The reason I would buy a new TV is to get the latest technology."

"I would buy a new pair of shoes because the new style is out."

"The new couch will look cool in my house."

An *away* person would respond to the same questions like this:

"I want a new TV because the old one is not doing the job."

"I would buy a new pair of shoes only if the old ones were out of style."

"A new TV? Only if the old one broke."

"I buy a couch only when the old one just doesn't do what I want it to do any more."

The difference between toward and away people is in their motivational direction. Toward people are motivated by pleasure, and away people are motivated by pain. Ultimately, the avoidance of pain is the most dominant motivator. Still, a given person has a specific motivational direction. How you assess the direction of each individual salesperson tells you how to effectively motivate each one. It is very hard to motivate an away person with praise, rewards, or learn-and-grow challenges. Away people really do not care about a contest for $5.00 a point for each roll of the dice. They do not really want to play and win. At the same time, they do not want to be left out and denied a roll of the dice. They don't want everyone but them winning money.

When toward people don't get a chance to roll the dice they don't care if they look bad. They want to roll and have fun and get the money and the rewards and the status that comes with the rolling of the dice. Same reward program, different motivational directions. Make sure you plan your motivations with both directions in mind.

Motivation is an interesting topic, and it could take volumes to cover it in depth. By understanding motivation, you know how to motivate others through praise, rewards, and learn-and-grow challenges. And you know how you can assist others in motivating themselves. Motivational direction—and knowing how to use it—is key to the success of any sales manager. Management is the ability to get things done through others, and how you effectively use motivational techniques is key. It starts with an understanding, then working through the S.O.S. Pyramid, M^{2}O/t's, and effectively applying these metrics every day.

A sales manager's job is to get things done through others. Understanding the other person's motivation, then using coaching and counseling techniques, provides the most effective way to empower employees to expand beyond their own paradigms. Successful coaching and counseling allows the salespeople to sell, which in turn allows the manager to do his job, which is managing the team to achieve the business objectives.

The choice is clear. If the manager has to do all the selling, there is no leverage and no need for effective management techniques. If the manager coaches and counsels his team, everyone does what is expected—and everyone wins.

Using Technology to Communicate

What would you do if you knew you could increase your communication skills 50 percent for less than $50.00? You could be better at communicating to your subordinates, peers, bosses, and customers for a small investment. Would you spend the money? Of course you would. So go buy a computer camera and install it on your laptop or desktop today.

Yahoo!, AIM, WebEx, Google, iChat, and a host of others allow you to v-mail or video-chat. If you want to be a better coach, use the technology that is proven to increase your ability to be understood. Your kids use it . . . why shouldn't you?

This will require you to change a process. It's just too easy to pick up the phone or shoot off an e-mail or IM. Get in the habit of having video meetings or video chats. You will be setting the standard, increasing communication comprehension, and getting less e-mail about what was covered. You can also record these meetings so that people who missed a meeting can catch up on their own time, not yours.

Mastering communication requires you to learn new skills and to work on listening and questioning. They are called skills for a reason: You can get better at them with practice. So go practice!

Chapter 7

If You Can't Measure It, Why Do It?

To be effective, a manager must manage to a quantifiable set of standards. This is important for many reasons; communication and expectations are just two of the more obvious ones.

Unfortunately, in some companies sales management tracks revenues only. There are two reasons for this: One, it is easy to get the revenue numbers; and two, it is the only scorecard against which most managers have ever measured. The following are typical comments heard all around the sales world:

> "Jim has a quota of $500,000 and he has sold $400,000 Y-T-D. So Jim is at 80 percent of his number."

> "Karen is at 112 percent of her number. She must be doing a great job."

> "Don has finished at 93 percent of the revenue plan."

The score is based on how well one performs against the revenue number. It has been measured this way for years. And what else would you use to keep score? What could be more telling than revenue? As we discovered in Chapter 3, revenue is a function of Frequencies and Competencies, or $R = F \times C$. This is how you objectively measure performance. But the ProActive sales manager must have something else in the toolbox to keep a step ahead of the game. In fact, there are two such tools: Track the Maybes and Keep the Insurance.

Track the Maybes

Yes and no decisions are great; it's the maybes that will kill you. Success in selling is tracked by revenue. It does not take a rocket scientist to figure out that the more deals you do, the more revenue you get, and the more successful you are. The sales management function even tracks these victories. Business-won reports, business-closed reports, and sales performance reports track sales victories. And business-lost reports track defeats. Sales managers are so busy tracking wins and losses they are forgetting the key to success: overcoming Maybes. Sales managers have been hearing this phrase, relative to business deals, all their sales lives:

> "Yeses are great, no's are bad, and Maybes are OK because you still have a chance."

This slogan has doomed many sales managers. The correct phrase really is:

> "Yeses are great, no's are great, and Maybes will kill you!"

Why? The buyer saying "Yes" to your proposal is obviously great since business is won.

The buyer saying "No" to your proposal is also great since it tells you that you are doing something wrong and you have the opportunity to fix it.

But "Maybe" means the buyer is undecided. Or leaning to the competition. Or that a delay is imminent. Or that the situation has developed to the point where "they are just not returning my phone calls." Maybes will kill you. All a Maybe does is sit in the sales funnel taking up time and limited resources.

A Maybe is a deal you are not in control of. *The buyer is always neutral.* If you are not in control of the sale and the buyer is neutral, guess who is in control of the sale. You got it: the competition. And competition does not necessarily mean your business rival. You're also competing against the customer doing nothing or spending the money elsewhere. Competition is anything that prevents you from getting the order!

A Maybe deal is one you end up funeral selling. Funeral selling is like funeral managing, which was discussed in Chapter 2, but from the sales perspective. Since your salesperson does not have control of the sale, you, the manager, get caught up and start funeral selling as well. You get called into the deal at the last minute and you end up asking something really clever like, "So, is there anything we can do?" Out of control of the sale. Funeral selling. The Maybes are in full force.

These Maybe deals typically represent 20 to 40+ percent of the deals in the sales pipeline. If left unchecked, they will hurt the careers of salespeople and sales managers. You need the salespeople to take ownership of the Maybes and have them decide, one way or another, if a deal is a deal and not a Maybe. We have to track Maybes. How do we do this? With the 30-60-90 report. But before we get to that we need to understand why we should add another report to those we already have.

Keep the Insurance

The last thing anyone needs is another report. We discussed one reason already: We need to find a way to track Maybes, since they are an important barometer of the existing sales funnel's health. The second reason is the concept of insurance policies.

Every good sales manager has taken out insurance to "make the number" for the year. By insurance we mean keeping some deals "in their pocket" or making a low forecast for that potential deal that will come in at two to three times the estimated amount. "Sandbagging" is a term often used to describe this phenomenon.

Sales managers have also been allowing the sales team to keep one of the more basic insurance policies: the forecast insurance policy. An example will help to illustrate.

A typical salesperson forecast is broken up into A, B, and C confidence factors, with A representing those deals the salesperson is most confident of achieving. In the sales forecast shown in Figure 7-1, the salesperson, Ron, is forecasting that he will exceed the quarterly quota by more than 6 percent. This is great, except the sales manager has allowed Ron to keep the insurance.

Figure 7-1. Sales funnel forecast by salesperson.

Salesperson: Ron Carson

	Forecast	*Factor*	*Total*
A Prospects			
Smith Co.	$100,000	90%	$ 90,000
Jones Corp.	75,000	90%	67,500
Davidson, Inc.	45,000	90%	40,500
B Prospects			
Johnson Corp.	$125,000	60%	$ 75,000
Great Co.	50,000	60%	30,000
Glass Inc.	55,000	60%	33,000
The A Co.	125,000	60%	75,000
ASSCO	200,000	60%	120,000
C Prospects			
Oniete Inc.	$500,000	20%	$100,000
Land One	110,000	20%	22,000
SDDTR	75,000	20%	15,000
Bocast Corp.	35,000	20%	7,000
Beckett Intl.	45,000	20%	9,000
Wills Co.	30,000	20%	6,000
		Forecast	$690,000
		Quarter Quota	$650,000
		% for Quarter	106.15%

For the manager to get the insurance back, let's look at the forecast insurance curve, as illustrated in Figure 7-2. The sales prospects are divided into forecast zones A, B, and C. It is a basic truism that as the actual number of prospective deals in the pipeline increases, the percentage of those that will turn into actual sales decreases. There are many reasons for this, such as deals just starting in the sales cycle, lack of sales ability, or lack of a definitive commitment from the buying organization. Statistically, it works out that salespeople have a few Zone A accounts, more Zone B accounts, and a lot of Zone C accounts.

Figure 7-2. Forecast insurance curve.

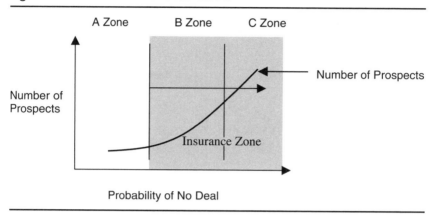

A problem occurs when sales management allows the sales-person to keep all the Zone A, Zone B, and Zone C prospects in her forecast when she should get to keep only Zone A prospects. The rest—Zone B and Zone C—is what we call the *insurance zone*. You need to keep Zone B and Zone C prospects—the insurance zone—for yourself, leaving the salesperson to forecast Zone A prospects.

In Ron's case, this would mean forecasting revenue of $198,000 against a quota of $650,000, or 30.5 percent of goal. The manager keeps the other zones as insurance.

You must take the responsibility for making quota off your back and place it on the salesperson. If you allow the salesperson to "get away" with forecasting the low probability Zone B and C deals, then you are taking on the responsibility and the risk—and the penalty if these low probabilities don't come in.

Give it back to the salesperson where it belongs. Let him forecast only A deals. Now in Ron's case, after he screams "unfair" for a while, he would probably go back and change a few things, such as taking the top three Zone B deals ($138,000) and adding them to the $198,000, for a total forecast of $336,000—still short of the $650,000 goal.

Now the questions that should be asked of Ron are:

"Ron, how will you make up the difference?"

"Ron, it seems like we have been a little lax on prospecting lately, eh?"

"Ron, I appreciate that you have a lot in your sales funnel. If you have a high degree of confidence that these deals are going to come in, then let's put them in Zone A, OK?"

The responsibility for making the number is now Ron's, not yours. More important, you get to keep the insurance policies in Zones B and C. Ron will have to put more energy into keeping Zone A high, which is what every sales manager wants their salespeople to do anyway.

This also changes the sales team's culture. It allows you to delegate sales forecasting to the responsible party—the salesperson. And it enables you to tell the salespeople not to forecast anything unless they have a high degree of confidence that they can make it happen.

Over time, the Zone A deals grow to meet the projected forecast. And you, as the sales manager, have taken out an even larger insurance policy. Now the forecast is swelling with Zone A prospects to meet the quota, and you still have the Zone B and C prospects as insurance.

Salespeople must be held accountable for their sales forecasts. Salespeople have a tendency to move Zone B and Zone C prospects into Zone A. But in a proper sales management review both parties must agree on genuine Zone A prospects. In that case the salesperson will have a better probability of success, and you'll both benefit from the insurance curve. It is a true win-win situation.

Manage to One Sheet of Paper: The 30-60-90 Report

Welcome to the 30-60-90 report, which forecasts the upcoming 30-60-90 days. It is your vehicle to track Maybes. Let's set up the rules, and then get to the report.

30-60-90 Rules

1. Sales managers must run the sales organization like a business. As such, they need timely ProActive reporting tools. What is timely? We believe you should do the following:

- Gather input weekly—get your details on a regular schedule.
- Adjust the forecast monthly—be able to spot trends sooner rather than later, and adjust your strategies accordingly.
- Reward on a quarterly basis—both positive and negative rewards, based on the circumstances. Formal quarterly rewards are a reminder to all on the state of the sales team's efforts.

2. The report must be mutually beneficial. A report that does not have value to both you and the salesperson will always be less effective and less useful than one that does.

3. Keep it simple. Keep it focused on what it was intended to accomplish. "I know it's sort of beside the point, but if we could add just one or two more things . . ." has killed many a report.

4. Use the 80/20 rule. This is a forecast report. Its value is in its timeliness. Salespeople should not have to forecast to the exact dollar amount. They just have to be close enough. Have a cutoff point on the forecast for deals under a certain dollar amount—anything you believe to be insignificant, say under $5,000 or $10,000. (This is another insurance policy for the sales manager anyway.)

5. The report must be easy for the salespeople to complete. It should take them no more than 15 minutes per week.

6. A neutral third party (such as a sales administrator or another sales manager) should control the input. Allowing the salesperson to update a report on a monthly basis gives her the liberty to take off a few Maybes when they are starting to look bad. The whole idea is to track the Maybes, not sweep them under the rug!

7. Reports must be submitted on a timely basis. Make it a rule: by noon on Friday, or whatever is appropriate for your company. Disciplinary action for failing to submit reports on time must be consistent, swift, and fair.

8. Once a line item on the report is completed, whether won or lost, the line item is removed and a new one, if applicable, is

inserted in its place. This report should not be used for Total Sales Y-T-D, Sales by Product Y-T-D, or anything Y-T-D. It is a rolling "balance sheet" report. You have other reports that provide you with Y-T-D information, such as Sales by Customer Y-T-D or Win/Loss reports. (A quick word on Win/Loss reports: Do not expect salespeople to be 100 percent truthful. Most of the time, when they lose a deal, it's because they were outsold. But that's not how they describe it in their Win/Loss reports. So, either take these reports with a grain of salt or don't bother with them at all.)

The 30-60-90 Report

The report itself is divided into three zones: A, B, and C. Only Zone A is eligible for forecasting against a quota. Zones B and C are only for the sales manager to view the sales pipeline. The key is that the salesperson must update the report weekly by doing one of three things:

1. Identifying business won. In the sample report shown in Figure 7-3, the salesperson has bolded the account dollar amount.
2. Identifying business lost, which is identified by an "x" in the report.
3. Identifying Maybes by placing a "$0" in the column for these accounts, the ones that keep slipping every month.

At the end of the month, the salesperson must choose what action (won, lost, or slip) needs to be recorded for the accounts on the report. "Won" is good, "lost" is good, and after a month or so, a "slip" is looking a lot like a Maybe. The salesperson must choose, not the manager. Responsibility for the accuracy of the forecast belongs at the salesperson's level.

In the report, you can also track where the salesperson is in the sales cycle of a certain account. The report shown in Figure 7-3 uses the sales cycle terminology of ProActive Selling, an M3 Learning sales program that lets the salesperson control the sales cycle and master qualification skills to eliminate Maybes. This enables focused communication between the salesperson and the sales manager. You can use this terminology or your own. The goal is to identify a sales process, keep it updated with duration times, and measure to it.

Figure 7-3 is an example of a good report. Now let's look at a report by a salesperson who is not doing well. As you can see in Figure 7-4, the report reveals problems:

- The large number of X marks indicates the business lost for which the salesperson had forecasted revenue. At the end of each month, the salesperson had to make a decision to either close, lose, or slip the forecasted deal. The forecasted sale could not just "vanish" from the list.

- The large number of slips ($0) indicates a low probability of "close" potential. These are Maybes or potential Maybes creeping into the forecast. This salesperson needs help in forecasting, and probably qualifying a potential deal. The Miller 17 should be used to highlight key areas of Frequency and Competency. Coaching can then begin on a ProActive basis instead of waiting a few months for a quarterly review.

- After three or four months, the slips, marked by a $0, obviously decrease in their probability of closing. A good rule of thumb is that if an account is on a 30-60-90 report for more than three months, it should be given an x and taken off the report or dropped to the B or C category.

Look at the duration time in each sale. Some have been in each stage way too long to be real deals. The manager can now coach to these items instead of "wishing" along with the salesperson that the deal's so close they can taste it.

After nine months, the report should look something like Figure 7-5.

A 30-60-90 weekly report allows you to take aggressive action on a monthly basis and reward on a quarterly basis accordingly. For some companies, it may be beneficial to do the report on a daily/weekly/monthly basis. For other situations, a monthly/quarterly/semiannual basis is acceptable. Some companies use units as a measure instead of dollars. Many companies use the report to track the top 20 percent of deals that bring

(*text continues on page 179*)

Figure 7-3. 30-60-90 Report: Debbie Jones.

Sales Person - Debbie Jones

Week End - February 26

ProActive Selling Sales Phase

1- Initial Interest	6- Validate
2- Educate	7- Propose
3- MMM	8- Close
4- Implementation Date	
5- Demonstration	

Bold - Business won
X - Business lost
$0 - Forecast slip

	Account	Product	Stage	Jan	Feb	Mar	Apr	May	Jun	Jul	Aug	Sep
Forecast	Account	Gas	6		$17,000			$34,000				
	Account	Gas	6	$55,900								
	Account	Light 1	6				$87,000					
	Account	Light 1	5		$0	$17,500						
	Account	Light 1	5			$33,000						
	Account	Inspector	7				$44,000					
	Account	Gadget	7			x	$30,000					
	Account	Gas	7	$0	$20,000							
	Account	Suite	6			$15,000						
	Account	Suite	6			$63,000						
	Totals by Month			$55,900	$37,000	$128,500	$161,000	$34,000	$0		$0	$0
	Totals by Quarter					$221,400			$195,000			$200,000
	Quota					$200,000			$200,000			$200,000
	% of Quota by Quarter					110.70%			97.50%			0.00%

FY 2000

(continues)

Figure 7-3. (continued).

Funnel

Account	Product		Jan	Feb	Mar	Apr	May	Jun	Jul	Aug	Sep
Account	Stopwatch	6		$16,700							
Account	Stopwatch	5				$63,000					
Account	Inspector	5		$0	$66,000						
Account	Gas						$44,800				
Account	Gas					$22,000					
Account	Gas					$21,900	$15,000				
Account	Gadget				$0						
Account	Stopwatch	4			$11,000						
Projected Totals			**$0**	**$16,700**	**$77,000**	**$106,900**	**$59,800**	**$0**	**$0**	**$0**	**$0**

Prospects

Account	Date Start	Status
Account	1-Jan	1
Account	1-Jan	1
Account	2-Jan	1
Account	2-Feb	2
Account	14-Feb	2
Account	28-Mar	1
Account	16-Mar	1
Account	13-May	2
Account	20-Apr	1
Account	1-May	1
Account	1-May	1

Figure 7-4. 30-60-90 Report: Bill Smith.

| Sales Person - Bill Smith |
| Week End - February 26 |

ProActive Selling Sales Phase		
1- Initial Interest	6- Validate	Bold - Business won
2- Educate	7- Propose	X - Business lost
3- MMM	8- Close	$0 - Forecast slip
4- Implementation Date		
5- Demonstration		

| | | | | | | | FY 2000 | | | | |
	Account	Product	Stage	Jan	Feb	Mar	Apr	May	Jun	Jul	Aug	Sep
Forecast	Account	Gas	6		$17,000							
	Account	Gas	6	$20,000								
	Account	Light 1	6	$15,000								
	Account	Light 1	5	x	$0	$0	$10,000					
	Account	Light 1	5		$0	$12,000						
	Account	Inspector	7	$0	x	$55,000						
	Account	Gadget	7			x	$30,000					
	Account	Gas	7	$0	$0	$0	$20,000					
	Account	Suite	6			$15,000	$12,000					
	Account	Suite	6									
	Totals by Month			$35,000	$17,000	$82,000	$72,000	$0	$0	$0	$0	$0
	Totals by Quarter					$134,000			$72,000			$0
	Quota					$200,000			$200,000			$200,000
	% of Quota by Quarter					67.00%			36.00%			0.00%

(continues)

Figure 7-4. (continued).

Funnel

Account	Product		Jan	Feb	Mar	Apr	May	Jun	Jul	Aug	Sep
Account	Stopwatch	6		$22,000							
Account	Stopwatch	5	x	x $0		$63,000					
Account	Inspector	5		$0	$66,000						
Account	Stopwatch	4									
Projected Totals			$0	$22,000	$66,000	$63,000	$0	$0	$0	$0	$0

Prospects

Account	Date Start	Status
Account	1-Jan	1
Account	1-Jan	1
Account	2-Jan	1
Account	2-Feb	2
Account	14-Feb	2
Account	28-Mar	1
Account	16-Mar	1
Account	13-May	2
Account	20-Apr	1
Account	1-May	1

Figure 7-5. 30-60-90 Report (after 90 days): Debbie Jones.

Sales Person - Debbie Jones		
Week End - September 26		

ProActive Selling Sales Phase

1- Initial Interest	6- Validate	Bold - Business won
2- Educate	7- Propose	X - Business lost
3- MMM	8- Close	$0 - Forecast slip
4- Implementation Date		
5- Demonstration		

FY 2000

	Account	Product	Stage	Jan	Feb	Mar	Apr	May	Jun	Jul	Aug	Sep
Forecast	Account	Gas	6		$17,000			$34,000				
	Account	Gas	6	$55,900					$45,000	$36,000		
	Account	Light 1	6				$87,000			$77,500		$0
	Account	Light 1	5		$0	$17,500						
	Account	Light 1	5			$33,000					$0	$26,000
	Account	Inspector	7				$44,000			$15,000		
	Account	Gadget	7			X	$30,000					
	Account	Gas	7	$0	$20,000					$0	$29,600	
	Account	Suite	6			$15,000				$42,000	$32,500	
	Account	Suite	6			$63,000						
	Totals by Month			$55,900	$37,000	$128,500	$161,000	$34,000	$45,000	$170,500	$29,600	$26,000
	Totals by Quarter					$221,400			$240,000			$226,100
	Quota					$200,000			$200,000			$200,000
	% of Quota by Quarter					110.70%			120.00%			113.05%

(continues)

Figure 7-5. (continued).

Funnel

Account	Product		Jan	Feb	Mar	Apr	May	Jun	Jul	Aug	Sep
Account	Stopwatch	6		x							$12,300
Account	Stopwatch	5			x		$0	$0	x		
Account	Inspector	5		$0	x						
Account	Gas									x	
Account	Gas						x	$0			x
Account	Gas						x	x			
Account	Gadget				$0						
Account	Stopwatch	4									$45,000
Projected Totals			$0	$0	$0	$0	$0	$0	$0	$0	$57,300

Prospects

Account	Date Start	Status
Account	1-Jan	1
Account	1-Jan	1
Account	2-Jan	1
Account	2-Feb	2
Account	14-Feb	2
Account	28-Mar	1
Account	16-Mar	1
Account	13-May	2
Account	20-Apr	1
Account	1-May	1
Account	1-May	1

in 80 percent of the revenue. Use any measurable unit, number of accounts, or time frame you feel you need to be successful. But make sure you track the Maybes.

Sales cycle duration is a key to this report. Measuring funnel speed is just as important as measuring what is in the funnel. Keep this one report up to date, and you will be getting much closer to 90 percent plus forecasting accuracy than you are today.

The 30-60-90 is one of the more controversial reports being used. It has been referred to as a "Big Brother Report" because it allows management to monitor salespeople. It has been called too cumbersome to use. In fact, it is a report that will take some time to set up and to get used to. However, a 30-60-90 report is the only way to:

- Give both parties timely input into the sales forecast method.
- Track performance by salesperson.
- Hold the right parties (salespeople) accountable.
- Identify failings (xs and $0s) ProActively.
- Combine a coaching tool with the Miller 17.
- Track the Maybes.

Remember, this is not a history-tracking report. You are forecasting the future. As such, you can forget about updating past months for exact dollar accuracy. It was designed as a tool to keep a future-based rolling 30-60-90 day forecast in line with expectations.

Try to keep it simple. You can add some additional items, like product type or sales cycle phase. Adding more items to it can make the report even more useful, but remember M^2O/t. If it is not *mutually* beneficial, it will not be effective.

A final note for sales management that uses distributors and independent agents (sales reps who do not work directly for the company): The 30-60-90 tool is a welcome addition since it keeps the business relationship in line with business expectations. If you are using distributors or independent rep firms to sell your products—depending on your company's commitment of resources, co-op advertising dollars, product training, or sales leads—the 30-60-90 is an acceptable measure of performance. You have a right to know how your investment is paying off, and how both parties can help keep the relationship a profitable one.

Another way to use a 30-60-90 report ProActively, according to Larry Freeman at SpectraLogic Corporation, is to encourage failure. "If a salesperson does not have any x marks on the report, I think he is not taking enough risks and is being too conservative. It's time we sat down and encouraged some more risk. Time to stretch the salesperson to fail. That's where the incremental deals are, and the difference between making quota and beating quota."

The 30-60-90. Use it to track the Maybes. Yeses are great, no's are great, and Maybes will cost you your job!

Effective Reports in Ten Minutes a Week

The 30-60-90 gives you a forecast report by an individual salesperson, which documents her predictions. If it is in a spreadsheet program such as Microsoft Excel, you can use the sum function to capture all the individual reports in a master forecast report, like the one shown in Figure 7-6.

This process, once set up in the computer, will take seconds. And it takes just minutes to apply your own weight factors to the forecast. For example, consider the following weight factors:

"Gail is a sandbagger. She is always conservative on the report. If I multiply her number by 1.15 every month, it is closer to the truth than what she gives me every month."

"Gene always forecasts high. Whatever his total is, if I multiply it by .8, I will get a much more accurate picture."

"Kim is almost always on the money. His number is an accurate picture of the forecast. I won't touch it."

Just think about generating a forecast in about 10 minutes a week. What a nice change. You can now use some time to be ProActive and plan your actions based on the forecast, rather than spending hours every week tracking down salespeople, or going over every deal line by line, trying to figure out which is

Figure 7-6. Team summary for 30-60-90 Report.

Northwest Sales Region

Week Ending June 23, 1999

Name	June	July	Aug.	Sept.
Doug				
Quota	$ 50,000	$ 60,000	$ 50,000	$ 40,000
Forecast	57,800	77,500	45,000	67,800
% of Quota	116%	129%	90%	170%
Bob				
Quota	$ 65,000	$ 55,000	$ 85,000	$ 40,000
Forecast	57,800	84,200	98,200	67,800
% of Quota	89%	153%	116%	170%
Gene				
Quota	$ 65,000	$ 48,000	$ 50,000	$ 65,000
Forecast	57,800	29,000	21,000	14,000
% of Quota	89%	60%	42%	22%
Larry				
Quota	$ 55,000	$ 60,000	$ 47,000	$ 39,000
Forecast	57,800	77,000	65,200	67,800
% of Quota	105%	128%	139%	174%
Gail				
Quota	$ 52,000	$ 61,000	$ 61,000	$ 61,000
Forecast	57,800	55,000	88,000	67,800
% of Quota	111%	90%	144%	111%
Kim				
Quota	$ 65,000	$ 65,000	$ 65,000	$ 65,000
Forecast	12,000	26,000	89,200	125,000
% of Quota	18%	40%	137%	192%
Jerry				
Quota	$ 56,000	$ 62,000	$ 44,000	$ 45,000
Forecast	68,000	78,000	46,300	62,100
% of Quota	121%	126%	105%	138%
Team Totals				
Quota	**$408,000**	**$411,000**	**$402,000**	**$355,000**
Forecast	**369,000**	**426,700**	**452,900**	**472,300**
% of Quota	**90%**	**104%**	**113%**	**133%**

real and which is not, or trying to determine which deal the salesperson took off the report and "forgot" to mention to you, or trying to give your boss your best educated guess. There are many ways you can spend your time reactively. It's time to spend it ProActively in just 10 minutes a week.

Getting Reports in on Time

A quick note on getting reports in on time. It seems there are some salespeople who do not like to adhere to the strict schedule of getting reports in at a certain time. Imagine that! They believe the rules are made for someone else, and, quite frankly, they are too busy getting revenue into the company right now and will get the report in during nonselling time, which almost always seems to be days after the due date.

Reports are a part of doing business. They do seem to be a difficult task for some to complete in a timely manner. How you handle the salespeople who are late with their reports will be directly related to your sales management style and will contribute to your team culture. What kind of sales manager are you when it comes to reports?

What Kind of a Manager Are You?

- The Laissez-Faire Manager—The salespeople will get it in when they get it in. They know their responsibilities.
- The Focused Manager—If the report has to be in by noon on Friday, then everything stops until the report is in.
- The General Patton Manager—One minute after the report is due, all hell breaks loose. It's better for the salesperson to get it in than to receive a visit from General Patton.
- The Gentle Reminder Manager—Consistently uses the gentle approach. Drops hints and hopes that enough hints and nudges will get the report completed in a timely manner.

- The Wimp Manager—Begs and pleads with the sales-people to get the report in as soon as they can. Stresses the difficulty of doing her job without the help and timely assistance from the salespeople. Would they kindly get the report in as soon as they find the time, please?
- The ProActive Manager—Sets processes in place to ensure timely responsiveness. Allows for "major" emergencies to delay input, but only on rare occasions. Assigns and delegates tasks to others for input if possible. Starts immediately using the report and its benefits and communicates its results so that the salespeople can understand why they have to do their job. The manager begins to coach and counsel immediately after the report is complete (input, *adjust*, reward). Penalties, if any, are defined up front so that the salesperson can decide if the report should be in on time.

Penalties may include:

- Being blocked from entering the office (or cubicle)
- A visit from the manager
- A call from the manager
- Having the employee's computer taken away
- Being locked out of voice mail/e-mail
- The posting of a "failure" list
- Reassignment of accounts
- Having a chair taken away in the office
- A visit to the boss's boss to remind the salesperson of the importance
- A call to the spouse at home

The list can go on. Some can be humorous and some can be pretty serious. Reports are an important part of the salesperson's job. Make sure that if a penalty is going to be used, it is used in a consistent and fair manner.

The other side of the coin is to exhibit a true ProActive manager quality by thanking the salespeople for getting the report in on time. People normally want to do a good job, and it's important to acknowledge when they do so. Leaders do not tell people what not to do. People already know what *not* to do. But they don't always know *what to do*. Leaders tell people what to do, and when the behavior matches the expectations, they remind them in a positive manner they have done a good job. Remember the 3 to 1 rule.

Expense Management

Tracking expenses is a task that must be accomplished by the sales team. Sales is required to obtain revenue for the company at a certain level of expenditure. If the cost of goods sold and the selling costs exceed the price of the product, a company will go out of business. Expense management is something that should not be taken lightly. Nor is it something that should be taken on by the sales management team alone.

Use objectives ($M^2O/t's$) to remind the salespeople of their responsibility to the corporation for watching over expenses. Items such as unnecessary travel and lavish dinners are not the only things we are talking about. Guidelines on excessive tipping, or on one-call trips that require out-of-town travel, should be spelled out in a travel expense guidebook. In such a guidebook, avoid terms that are open for interpretation, such as "common sense should be used" or "reasonable." Be specific, such as "tipping of no more than 15 percent will be allowed" or "individual travel reports over $x will require that a salesperson make a minimum of x sales calls." How you enforce this policy is up to your sales team culture. Expense management should be delegated down to the salesperson level, and it can even be a part of total compensation.

A travel guidebook allows you to stop being reactive on expense reports and tells the salespeople what is expected of them before they spend the money. The ProActive Sales Manager strikes again!

Chapter 8

Territory Planning, Compensation, and Rewards

For ProActive sales management tools to work, you must plan a strategy and then execute to it. To plan a strategy for your sales team, you must consider two factors: The first is how to deploy the sales team strategically, and the second is how to maximize the salesperson's time to bring in the largest dollar volume.

Strategically Deploying the Sales Team

There are three approaches to the strategic deployment of a sales team:

1. *Geographic Assignments*: Many sales organizations divide up a territory by state, region, county, zip codes, or however it makes the most sense at the time. Geographic organization is usually the easiest and cleanest way to divide a sales territory.
2. *Account Assignments*: Dividing up a territory by named accounts or by named industries is also a clean way to manage a sales team when there are some large accounts that need coordination across territories.
3. *Product Assignments*: Organizing by product means letting certain salespeople focus on selling designated

products. This is a good way to manage sales territories when product specialization is necessary and the salesperson has to provide quite a bit of product value add. Product specialization is also a way many companies push low-end products to gain market penetration.

As illustrated in Figure 8-1, each type of organization has advantages and disadvantages. Most companies have a combination of all three types. How to align the sales territories strategically based on future needs is another topic altogether. But be aware of the three types, do a FutureVision or an S.O.S. Pyramid, and go for it. The most important thing to address: how to maximize your salespeople's time to bring in revenue.

The ProActive Sales Matrix

The ProActive Sales Matrix is a way for you and the salesperson mutually to define where to deploy her most precious resource:

Figure 8-1. Types of sales territories.

Type of Sales Territory	Pros	Cons
Geographic	Easy, Clean, and Minimal Disputes Less Travel Cost Deeper Geographical Penetration	Less Specialization Less Customer Continuity Constant Change with Growth
Account	High Customer Centric Deep Industry Penetration High in Relationship Selling Maximizes 80/20 Rule	Higher Travel Budgets Less Geographic Coverage Low New Account Focus
Product	High Value-Add Sale Approach Adaptable to Fast-Changing Products Market Penetration	Less Relationship Selling Less Customer Focus Can Get Complex

time. The goal of sales management is to reduce its risk. The goal of salespeople is to maximize time and opportunities. Both can be accomplished with the ProActive Sales Matrix.

The matrix adds a new dimension to the sales forecast. Typically, a salesperson forecasts the current opportunities in an A-B-C type of forecast.

• A—The current hot prospects. The accounts the salesperson is banking on. A 90 percent likelihood factor is typically assigned to these prospects.

• B—The medium prospects. Typically, these accounts are in the funnel and are considered work in process. A 60 to 70 percent likelihood factor is usually assigned to these prospects.

• C—The lukewarm prospects. More than likely, these are the prospects just being qualified, the prospects that are just starting in the sales cycle, or the "hope and a prayer" prospects. A 20 to 40 percent likelihood factor is usually applied to these accounts.

Figure 8-2 shows a typical A-B-C type of sales forecast. This is exactly the same input we used for the 30-60-90 report discussed in Chapter 7. Although there can be many variations in a sales funnel report, if we treat this example as typical, we can see where the ProActive Sales Matrix can help.

From the sales manager's point of view, there are some flaws in the type of reporting shown in Figure 8-2. The sales manager has allowed the salesperson to include the medium and lukewarm prospects in the forecast. The manager has then adjusted the salesperson's forecast by using percentage factors to gauge his own risk. This is reactive sales planning.

A forecast like this tells you what the salesperson has done, not what he is about to do. It reports on activities that have brought this account to its current status and then takes a stab at the probability of future activity and potential. In a typical forecast like this, 80 to 90 percent of the probability is based on what *sales activities have been done in the past*, and about 10 to 20 percent of the probability is based on *what the future activity is*. These percentages need to be reversed!

Figure 8-2. Sales forecast.

Salesperson: Ron Carson

	Forecast	Factor	Total
A Prospects			
Smith Co.	$100,000	90%	$ 90,000
Jones Corp.	75,000	90%	67,500
Davidson, Inc.	45,000	90%	40,500
B Prospects			
Johnson Corp.	$125,000	60%	$ 75,000
Great Co.	50,000	60%	30,000
Glass Inc.	55,000	60%	33,000
The A Co.	125,000	60%	75,000
ASSCO	200,000	60%	120,000
C Prospects			
Oniete Inc.	$500,000	20%	$100,000
Land One	110,000	20%	22,000
SDDTR	75,000	20%	15,000
Bocast Corp.	35,000	20%	7,000
Beckett Intl.	45,000	20%	9,000
Wills Co.	30,000	20%	6,000
		Forecast	$690,000
		Quarter Quota	$650,000
		% for Quarter	106.15%

What is missing from this typical forecast is a ProActive view, a view into future activities. To do this, we need to add a dimension to the forecast method to tell the salesperson as well as the manager that the salesperson is ProActive and has confidence in what activities he needs to do next.

The ProActive Sales Matrix allows the manager to effectively communicate to the sales team on a consistent basis what is needed and what is important. It does this by adding a new dimension to the A-B-C forecast method: a second letter-symbol.

By adding a second letter to the matrix, we now have an

AA prospect instead of an A prospect. The first letter stands for current or past activity of the account, and the second signifies the account's future activity. Additionally, the letter itself signifies the dollar amount (or other measurable unit) that is being evaluated (Figure 8-3).

The letters must represent dollar figures. You can use whatever dollar amounts make sense for your sales environment. For example:

A—Sales greater than $100,000
B—Sales between $30,000 and $100,000
C—Sales less than $30,000

Thus, the two letters represent both time and dollar amounts. Let's also assume a sales forecast window of 90 to 120 days.

So an AA account is one that has spent more than $100,000 with us in the past or currently (AA), and that has the potential in the next 90 to 120 days to spend over $100,000 with us (AA). CA prospect status would mean that the account currently or in the past has spent less than $30,000 (CA) and has the potential in 90 to 120 days to spend more than $100,000 (CA). Now we know where we should be spending our time.

Figure 8-3. The ProActive Sales Matrix.

Old Method of Forecasting		ProActive Method of Forecasting		
A		AA	AB	AC
B		BA	BB	BC
C		CA	CB	CC

Dead Zone

The Dead Zone is where salespeople typically spend 60 to 80 percent of their time. But it should be just 10 to 25 percent. This zone is filled with customers calling in with problems or questions, who currently offer very little potential for additional business. Since salespeople are reacting to customer requests, this is considered reactive selling time. The 80/20/80 rule applies here. Approximately 80 percent of the customers generate 20 percent of the revenue as well as 80 percent of the problems! There are customers in this zone we should actually consider not even having as customers (Figure 8-4).

Maintain Zone

The Maintain Zone, also called the Comfort Zone, is composed of customers who are important to us—the bread and butter of the territory. They have spent a lot of money with us in the past. However, we should not spend a whole lot of time here right now. Their current budget or buying window does not require a lot of our time. Yes, there is business to be had, but there is better use of our short-term time and resources. We should spend 10 to 20 percent of our time here. Why do salespeople spend more than that amount of time here? Because these people are their friends and they feel comfortable calling on them,

Figure 8-4. A complete ProActive Sales Matrix.

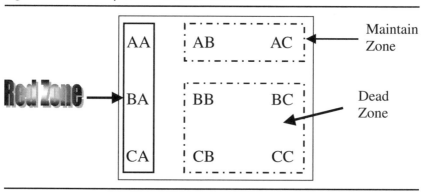

seeing them again, or just hanging out with them. There is no short-term financial gain, but it's better than having to prospect for *new* business.

Red Zone

The Red Zone comprises prospects that have the potential to spend a lot of money with us in a short period of time. We need to invest time in this zone. This is the case especially in the BA and CA zones, because these are accounts that have a large enough potential to justify spending precious time with, like on a new major deal that the competition is going to lose. If the salespeople want to spend their time in the other zones, fine. Just be aware that Zone BA and CA deals are happening, and they are probably being awarded to one of your competitors.

Why is it hard to call on these BA and CA Red Zone accounts? As with Maintain Zone accounts, it would involve *prospecting*, and we all know how much salespeople love to prospect! Red Zone accounts should be identified, and 20 to 40 percent of our time should be ProActively spent here. PowerHour time would be a good start.

Additionally, another option for the matrix is for you to designate the second letter to represent future time. The first signifies today. For the second, let's assume the following time spans:

A—within 90 days
B—between 90 and 180 days
C—greater than 180 days

If you use the time variable in place of the dollar variable for the second letter, then an account labeled as BB is a customer who has spent a fair amount of money with you in the past (B), and will be an active prospect in the next 90 to 180 days (B).

You could also use three variables by adding a numerical digit (1, 2, 3) to represent time. For example, an AA1 would be a customer who has spent more than $100,000 with you in the past, and who has the potential of spending $100,000 with you within 90 days. This is an added level of complexity, however, and you may be better off staying with just two variables.

An example will help to explain the Matrix more clearly.

Jane wanted to look ProActively at her account base and figure out where she should be spending her time. She classified as A accounts those with revenue potential of $100,000 or more. Revenue potential for B accounts was from $25,000 to $100,000, and for C accounts from $10,000 to $25,000. Any accounts below $10,000 she kept off the forecast.

By using the ProActive Sales Matrix, Jane and her boss:

- Looked at her Day Timer and reviewed her schedule 0 to 90 days out. They noted her appointments and where she was planning to spend her time.

- Decided that she was going to spend 40 percent of her time in the Red Zone.

- Used M²O/t to determine where she needed to be.

Both Jane and the sales manager agreed on the calls she would make. She turned over some of her calls to the customer support team, postponed a visit to an AC account, and got rid of two BC Maybe accounts. She and her manager are focusing on profitable, timely business. They're being ProActive.

The ProActive Sales Matrix allows the manager to assist the salespeople as they plan their time and resources. Rather than focus on what they did in the past, it gives the salespeople an objective view of what they are doing now, and what they need to do to ensure their future success. It allows the manager to ProActively assess what activities are going on in the territory, whether the correct amount of resources is being applied to the right accounts, and how much risk the territory is taking. It also gives the manager an objective communications tool to discuss frequencies and competencies with the sales team.

If the sales team is planning effectively and working Fs and Cs into the plan, they will get their rewards. Rewards can be in multiple formats, such as praise, recognition, and the learn-and-grow plan. Another reward that needs to be addressed is compensation.

Compensation

Earlier, when we discussed motivation, we pointed out that pay was not the motivator some of us thought that it was. We noted that praise, rewards, and the learn-and-grow plans motivate top performers. It is with this reminder that we now cover compensation.

Compensation is the ultimate measure. In the final analysis, salespeople are more likely to fight over compensation issues than nearly anything else. And not just for pay or money reasons per se, but because they feel compensation is the true measure of their success. To them, it's the final score that tells them how well they are doing across industry boundaries.

Strategic vs. Tactical Compensation

There are two kinds of compensation: strategic and tactical. *Strategic* compensation is what we think of when we discuss annual compensation plans, territories, and any long-term monetary decision. *Tactical* compensation takes the form of contests, bonuses, rewards, and programs that are meant to have a short-term impact on a specific part of the business. Examples would be a contest to get sales moving in a certain product area, a bonus payment for a specific task accomplished, or a program that carries with it some degree of recognition.

Strategic programs are designed with the company's long-term viability in mind. An S.O.S. should be taken each year to determine what long-term compensation issues are right for the business at that given time, and how much money should be allocated to each salesperson in the form of base pay, commission, and bonus payments.

ProActive Compensation Guidelines

In general, a compensation program should be designed with the following guidelines in mind:

• *Be specific.* The more specific the compensation program, the clearer your communication about it will be. Try to minimize exceptions in the compensation plan. If you make it overly complicated, salespeople will try to figure out how to make it work for them—perhaps even in ways you hadn't planned. Focus on the needs of the company and determine how you want to compensate. Keep it simple.

• *Be fair.* Many organizations can get a little stingy in their compensation plans. Then they wonder why salespeople stop working when they get to 100 percent of their quota. Many companies pay for performance, and then hold out a small carrot for their salespeople to overachieve their numbers. This is not smart. The saying is "Play for pay." If salespeople overachieve their plan, pay them for it. The more they surpass their quota—as long as it is in the company's best financial interest—the better for all. Pay for play organizations tend to keep their A players. Stingy organizations tend to lose them.

• *Lower the risk.* Putting an aggressive compensation plan together and putting a "cap" on how much the salesperson can earn is acceptable. All this "I would never work in an environment where there is a cap" talk is nonsense. If at the end of the year, you assess the risk, and you want to lift the cap, lift it. A cap is for minimizing the company's risk. You can change the rules on the cap and still be fair.

A management catch phrase at the end of the compensation plan such as "All decisions and interpretations of this compensation plan are the sole discretion of management" is also acceptable to cover any unanticipated situations that may arise. Companies are supposed to cover their risk. Sales management should produce a sales compensation plan that is acceptable to the sales team and that puts the company at minimal risk.

• *Be focused.* The details of how you pay salespeople and the sales management team are another subject in itself. The issues are simple, but the workings can get very complex. However, for a compensation plan to work, there are three macro issues on which the senior sales management team needs to focus.

1. *A split between base pay and total compensation.* This is a risk assessment and a pure judgment call. Typical ratios of 60/

40, 40/60, or even 80/20 base pay/commission at 100 percent of plan are standard. (The first number is the percentage of base pay, and the second number is variable compensation. Thus, the 60/40 plan means that the salesperson receives 60 percent of total compensation in base pay and the rest in commissions and bonuses.) The more risky the company's proposition, the more you may have to give in base pay. The less the base pay, the more risk for the salesperson. The general rule is that when you have top performers, you should pass the risk and the rewards to them. When you do not have a high percentage of top performers and when you are in a minimal growth market, then lower the sales team's risk and rewards.

2. *Types of commission.* Commissions come in many forms, such as:

- Percent of overall revenue
- Percent of overall profit
- Percent of revenue by product
- Percent of profit by product
- Percent of quota
- Bonus payments for tasks completed (typically called management by objectives, or MBOs)
- Strategic contests throughout the year (in anticipation of a third-quarter "slump," a second-quarter contest to prime the pump is budgeted and planned for)
- Stock options

There are numerous ways to compensate. Stay focused on the company's overall objectives. Do not focus on objectives solely to the benefit of the salesperson, or do whatever is easier, or create "we-have-always-done-it-this-way-before" objectives. Play FutureVision, create your S.O.S. Pyramid, establish your M²O/t's, and see whether the compensation plan fulfills the objectives. If so, that's great. If not, get it focused!

3. *Compensation per salesperson.* A ProActive sales manager divides the salesperson compensation into three categories: salary, commission, and bonus.

- *Salary* is the part of the total compensation that the salesperson receives as a weekly, semimonthly, or monthly base pay. This amount is usually a percentage of the total compensation.

- *Commission* is the reward for salespeople bringing profitable business to the company.

- *Bonus* is the amount of discretionary money you can use for contests, quick reward programs, and the like. This is a key variable that can be used to reward A players (who usually win the contests and bonus programs anyway). Many companies are now forgoing annual base pay raises for the sales staff and allocating this money to bonus programs. A good rule of thumb is to allocate 10 percent of total compensation for these types of bonus programs.

- *Be honest.* This among all things is key. It pays to designate a neutral third party—human resources, the chief financial officer, or someone else in the company—as the ombudsman, someone you can ask for advice during a compensation dispute. Both the salesperson and the sales manager can be too close to the situation, and a third perspective is often a welcome addition.

- *Be the salesperson.* This may sound obvious, but make sure you look at the compensation from the salesperson's perspective. Would this be a compensation program that would keep *you* motivated? Is it fair? Is it favoring the company too much? Is it favoring a certain product that is noncompetitive? Is there a high commission on certain products just because the company wants to sell them or dump them and the market thinks otherwise? Is there enough risk/reward for both parties? Is it too complicated? Are there too many question areas open for interpretation? You may want to run the compensation program past a few good salespeople. Get their opinion and early buy-in before you announce it. Think a little like a salesperson and you will see things from a different perspective, which in most cases is a good thing. Balance this perspective with your own in making compensation decisions.

- *Be the company.* From the company perspective, a compensation program should address the following questions:

1. Is the program manageable? Does the compensation program require a Ph.D. to administer? Is it simple and straightfor-

ward? Is it too full of legalese? Can it be communicated in one page? This is a good test, even if your company has thousands of employees. The more complex the program is to administer, the more it is going to cost the company in resources, time, and money to interpret it for the salespeople. Keep it simple. Add complexity if needed on a tactical basis, with contests and bonuses. Keep the body of the strategic compensation plan as simple as possible.

2. Does it keep employees motivated? Is there enough reward for the top salespeople? If the A salespeople overachieve, will the company pay for this performance? Is there enough carrot to keep the top salespeople challenged?

3. Does it keep the employee an employee? Is the compensation program too easy for a salesperson to cash out? Paying weekly commissions or paying the entire commission when the order is signed may not be in the company's best interest. If you are in an industry where top salespeople have opportunities around every corner, one thing that must cross their minds before they leave a company is, "How much money am I leaving on the table?" To pay salespeople immediately after a sale may be the right thing for your industry, but consider leveraging your compensation program over time to keep an employee an employee.

Another reason to do this is to lower the company's risk. If a salesperson takes the commission and then leaves the company, who is going to maintain the customer? Will the next person be happy to work with a new customer, say get the customer up to speed on what they purchased, but without getting fully compensated for it? Commissions are not just for getting a sale; they must be seen from a company perspective and structured for the entire life of the sale, not just for the signature on the dotted line. The company risk has to be taken into consideration as well.

• *Be ProActive.* The ProActive sales manager does not settle for keeping things the way they have always been. Here are some important trends: compensating salespeople by margin to allow them the responsibility and the authority for discounts;

paying a premium for new business over business from current customers, or for breaking new products into new markets; and dedicating an e-business sales team and leveraging their objectives and compensation to the rest of the sales organization.

Whoever coined the phrase "Whatever got you to where you are today is not good enough to get you where you need to be" had to be thinking about compensation plans. Compensation plans should be changed annually, with overall reviews and major modifications every three years. Your business has changed a lot in three years, hasn't it? The next three years will bring as much change, if not more. Your compensation plan should reflect that.

From a tactical standpoint, compensation programs must allow for flexibility. They must be open to allow tactical contests and programs to achieve the overall company goal. You must be able to tactically adjust to market conditions and sales situations that arise during the year and have the tools to motivate the members of the sales team in the direction they want it to go. Examples of these types of programs are:

- Sales contests to get new business.
- Contests to spur on sales in a certain product area.
- Resources for quarterly parachute drops: A *parachute drop* is a program designed to spur on sales in a new territory, one that is being handled by a new salesperson, or just a slow moving territory. You choose what territory to blitz, and then you "parachute" a sales team into the territory for a day or two. As a team and as individuals, they prospect the heck out of the territory. These programs are surprisingly fun and very effective.
- Blitz Days are when salespeople blitz a sales territory— either their own or someone else's, usually by phone. Themes can be used, such as a golf tournament or a car race. Payoffs are on topics such as most calls attempted, most presentations made, most presentations to a vice president, or most face-to-face appointments made.
- Reward programs. The Roll-the-Dough contest mentioned before falls into this category. The first to close a sale in excess of $x would get a reward. Model it after an airline fre-

quent flyer program and offer certain prizes after so many points. Reward incentives, such as letterman jackets with merit badges, are still effective.

Tactical programs are focused on an S.O.S. analysis of the sales situation and a determination of what is needed by the sales organization over the next three months. These programs should then be implemented a few months before you want results. Tactical programs cannot affect business in the very near term, unless you offer additional discounts or give away more for the same amount. Price is usually the only weapon that can bring in business or revenue in the short term. After all, if it can be sold over the next few weeks, a salesperson would be selling it. Therefore, a tactical program would not speed up the sale or make the customer sign any earlier. You want to think two to three months ahead for your tactical programs and ProActively design them so they affect the future. The future is where the A players are playing, and where the ProActive sales manager should be as well.

Compensation and Territory Timing

Speed is a dangerous game. Go too fast and you burn up. Go too slow and you'll be left in the dust. Making quick decisions and making the right decisions were never more at odds. Here is some input for your decisions on compensation.

The annual compensation plan is dead.

That's right. Turning battleships is a thing of the past. Quarterly and even monthly compensation plans and territory assignments are getting more and more popular for their ability to:

- Pay for the right activity in a timely manner.
- Get the right salespeople on the right accounts in a timely manner.

"I knew I had the wrong sales person on the account. It just took me nine months to make the switch."

"If Jane had that territory, I knew I would be 20 percent ahead. I had to wait until the start of the fiscal year to pull it off."

"To make that kind of compensation switch, it would require me moving mountains, and I don't know if that is really worth the fight."

It's worth the fight.

Give salespeople 20 accounts per quarter, and at the end of the quarter, you take their current accounts and their new accounts and let them pick 20 out of that group. The ones that fall out go to the inside sales team, the new salespeople, or the e-sales group.

Make the compensation 30 percent quarterly variable. This way, salespeople can focus on quarterly numbers rather than annual numbers. It's rare to find a salesperson who doesn't look at the annual number and then rationalize their "poor" work in the first few months of the year. "Catching up" is something you do not want a sales team doing three or four months into a fiscal year.

All of this leads to the law of compensation.

Compensate for activities, not results.

It's better to reward the right activity than it is to reward just results. You want your sales team doing the right things to get the desired results. It's not just about rewarding on "closed business," and not caring how the business got closed.

Along those lines is the proverbial sales manager's concern: "John is a C+/B− player at best, and has had the ABC account for six years. Do I keep him on it? He is getting good revenue, knows all the people, and they like him. What should I do?"

The answer is:

1. Give John some M²O/t's to get him prospecting to new divisions and new projects.
2. Replace John as quick as you can with an A player.

Unless you keep John motivated, he's not going to prospect for new business when he can get business out of his friends at ABC. A new person who has no friends will quickly find out who has the power, regardless of past relationships. Most managers make the switch, and then wonder why it took them so long. And you cannot have this type of decision making with an annual compensation plan.

Get your metrics around compensation and territory faster. It is too important to have just "out there" and only get a chance to work on it once a year.

Finally, do not make the compensation plan a work of art. One page works fine. The simpler, the better. If you are going to increase speed, cut the complexity or you will have salespeople figuring out the comp plan—figuring out when *not* to sell! One page is best.

The Law of Compensation Plan Timing

Compensation plan timing has an unwritten law that while straightforward and simple is often misunderstood or just plain forgotten. This law states that *the sooner the compensation plan is in the hands of the sales team, the sooner they will start to sell.*

Salespeople treat their territory like their own business. Management encourages this to keep the salespeople's motivation high and keep them customer-focused. At the beginning of the new fiscal year, they expect to be given their goals and objectives for their territory, for the business that they manage.

Salespeople will not sell until they have their goals and objectives. They will begin selling only when they get their compensation package and quota. If your fiscal year begins in January, you need to deliver their quota and compensation plan by the first week in January. Any later and you will run the risk of getting behind the revenue curve.

The Revenue Curve

The revenue curve concept is one where you, as the sales manager, have 12 months to make an annual number. If your year kicks off in January, you need to close the business that was forecasted to come in during that month. February business should close in February, March in March, and so on. You get behind the revenue curve when you start slipping against the forecast. It starts to snowball. You close as much business as you can in January; you do the leftover January business and some February business in February; and you do the final January, some February, and some March business in March. By the time you get to November, you are closing the September business, and you are well behind the revenue curve.

If you don't give the salespeople their quota until, say, February 1, they will not start selling until February 1. You will be behind the revenue curve. If, on the other hand, you give the salespeople their quota before the end of the year, they will stop focusing on the end-of-year objectives that the company wants them to pursue. Another reason to increase speed of comp plan metrics.

At this point, sales and top management say, "Salespeople sell. Why do they need a quota to sell? Just go sell as much as you can. We'll get you your final quota and compensation plan as soon as we can." This is a behind-the-revenue-curve situation waiting to happen.

Management is being reactive and still deciding what the quota should be, what the distribution should be, and how to pay the sales team. While they are doing that, the salespeople are not selling. The quota clock is ticking, and the revenue curve is getting larger. Management believes the salespeople are selling. But they're not. Salespeople are goal-oriented; management has trained them to be that way. Without a goal, without their quota, they may do some farming work, some administrative work, or even answer some phone calls. But they won't hunt for new business.

Worse, if the salespeople even think that with the new annual quota there may be even a slight chance of territory realignment or compensation adjustment, you have just shut down the entire sales force. Gossip and rumor-mongering increase while selling decreases.

Be ProActive in the timing of the quotas, compensation plans, and territory assignments. Have them out to the salespeople within five business days of the start of the quota time frame. As hard as it is for management to believe, salespeople will not give 100 percent effort until they receive and understand their objectives.

Get the salespeople selling as soon as you can, even if you have to give them preliminary information that may change in a week or so. Time waits for no one. Unless you are ProActive you will have a difficult time making up for lost selling days. Get the sales team selling as soon as possible. It's hard to make a 12-month number in 10 or 11 months. Get them their objectives, quota, compensation plan, and assigned territory as early as you can. Give them 12 months to make a 12-month number. Getting behind the revenue curve will double the effort you will need to make the annual goal. You are given a year to make the number. Take the whole year! Get the salespeople the information they need in the first week—turn the sales team loose.

Stack Rankings

Stack rankings, tote boards, leader boards, and sales thermometers all have one thing in common: They highlight the good and the bad, the top performers and the laggards. Whether to use a stack ranking system or not, that is the question. Again, turn to your S.O.S. Do you want the positive and the negative outcome that is associated with a stack ranking? It makes the leaders look great, but does it negatively impact the trailers? Is your business one where C players may lead in the stack ranking because their quota is only one third of your A players? If so, would that have a reverse effect on your top performers? Or is your business one where A players really perform and where stack ranking would highlight their actual contributions?

In general, stack rankings are a good idea. Praise, reward, and recognition are strong motivators, and positive publicity is always a good thing. Salespeople generally want an idea of how they are doing. And they want everyone to know when they are doing well. So, if you are undecided, try it. It is amazing sometimes how a little positive/negative stroke can spur on a rush of activity.

You know that a program is successful when a top performer uses it as a guideline for success. A vice president of sales relates the following story:

A top salesperson was stack-ranked #3 out of twenty-seven salespeople at the end of the year. When the finance department released the final numbers two months after the year end, he finished #2 by .003 percent. He requested that the previous year's stack rankings be republished and distributed to everyone. He had finished #2, and he wanted everyone to know. Do some salespeople take stack rankings seriously? Well, he did, and he has always been a top performer.

Sales Training

The Five Sales Competencies

How can you increase the competencies of your sales team? What training should you invest in? When should you invest? How often should you invest in your salespeople? The answers revolve around the five sales competencies.

1. *Product Knowledge*: Information about the goods or services being sold.
2. *Selling Skills*: Sales cycle control, qualifying skills, value creation ability. These are the basics of selling.
3. *Communication Skills*: Behavior profiling, neuro-linguistic programming skills, and effective listening and negotiating skills, to name a few.
4. *Presentation Skills*: Over-the-phone, in-person, and group presentation skills.
5. *Personal Growth*: Personal confidence, learning and growing skills.

These are the five sales competencies. Sales managers must S.O.S. the sales organization and develop their training plans around these five areas. Too often it happens that sales management brings in the sales team for three or four days of intensive sales training, only to allocate 90 percent of the available time to product knowledge. The rest of the time gets allocated to a sales success story or two, a brief subjective competitive assessment, a 60-minute motivational speaker, or anything else anyone can think of in the hopes that something good will rub off. Sales training is analogous to a bicycle.

A bicycle has three areas: the front wheel, the back wheel, and the frame that holds the bicycle together. The back wheel provides power to the bike, similar to what product knowledge provides to a salesperson. The front wheel provides steering and direction, similar to the selling, presentation, and communication skills we discussed. The frame is the environment, the piece that holds it all together. This is the sales culture, which can be influenced by team-building events, personal growth courses, and other programs that you can implement. Now the trick is to decide what to do. S.O.S. it. What does your sales team need the most over the next three to six months? Product knowledge only? Not likely.

An army general who goes into battle with poorly trained soldiers is asking for defeat. A conductor of a world-class symphony orchestra always evaluates each member of the orchestra when considering playing a new type of music and makes sure they are fully trained to perform it. The football coach needs to assess every player at every position relative to the next opponent and make sure he is fully prepared to have the best chance of winning.

When you invest in training your sales team and cover all five sales competencies, you send them out fully armed for battle. You will get the desired results, and in the right priority. Take an assessment of your current sales team and determine what skill set(s) they need to increase the probability of success. Whatever the answer is, invest 50 percent of your annual sales-training budget to accomplish that goal. What if you do not have a sales-training budget? You can do one of three things.

1. *Get one.*
2. *Fake it.* Buy books for the sales team and cover a chapter per week. Start the weekly sales meeting by having one salesperson cover a sales-training topic. Create a weekly

quiz to test people's knowledge in certain sales areas—and make it fun! Do whatever it takes to make the sales team smarter.

3. *Find another job.* The battle is won or lost before the first shot is fired. If you are going to market with a sales staff poorly trained in the five sales competencies, the results are predictable.

You can train once a week, once a month, twice a year—it does not really matter as long as you abide by the results of your S.O.S. The only thing that does matter is that you invest in your people in a ProActive way, around the five sales competencies. There are too many stories of sales managers who have not invested in their people and wonder why the results have not come in. There are also stories of sales managers who have invested in their people and are winning.

Karen Bocast, sales vice president of a division of Sterling Software, a major software company, was promoted at the beginning of the fiscal year. "I did an S.O.S. and assessed we needed help in four of the sales competency areas," Karen said. For the entire first month of the year, she had her salespeople in training all but two selling days of the month. That's right, during the first month of her new job, she only gave her salespeople two days to sell. The rest of the time, she invested in helping them gain product knowledge, selling skills, negotiation skills, communication skills, and presentation skills—all in a single month. It became a team-building event. Risky? Sure, but her S.O.S told her she had to get her sales team's competencies up.

Although not a popular decision with her top management at the time, Karen did the right thing. "I now have a team that is highly skilled in all sales competencies, knows what they are doing, and believes they can win." The results are predictable. She caught up and even passed the revenue curve. Her division went right to the top, a distinction it never had before she got there. This is the predictability of working with the five sales competencies. Bottom line: Twelve months later she was promoted to president. ProActive sales training really does work.

A final note: Some managers have asked if the five sales competencies fit into the Miller 17. Of course they do. Based on your S.O.S., you can apply the competencies that you feel are needed.

Create Leverage—Rewards and Praise

The idea of rewards can be a costly investment if not done right. The size of the reward is second to the amount of attention you put on it. To do it right you do not have to spend a lot of resources, time, and money. You need to leverage the situation.

Leveraging is accomplished not by the size of the reward, but by the focus and attention the sales manager puts on the reward program. A $1,000 check presented without fanfare makes much less of an impact than a $100 bill presented with a lot of hoopla. You can gain leverage in many ways.

- One company had a reward program for sales leader per quarter. The sales manager purchased DVD players, Dolby Digital receivers, 35-inch television sets, and other electronic equipment. He put the prizes on display so that everyone had a daily reminder of what they could walk away with at the end of the quarter.

- One manager, knowing that all of his salespeople liked to play golf, used a new driver, a new putter, and new golfing apparel as prizes. He claims his best idea was golf for two at the famous Pebble Beach Golf Course in California. Each prize cost him from $100 to $1,000. The sales team loved it.

- Another program involved event tickets. The winner of the month was awarded four tickets (in the first ten rows) to sporting events, concerts, plays, or the circus. The manager claims the costs were very reasonable for the results obtained. The favorite prizes were a Rolling Stones concert (including limousine) and four tickets to a World Series game.

There are hundreds of possible awards that are reasonably priced and can have a tremendous impact. Other ideas for internal usage include:

• A leader board with digital photos. Put a face to the name and the board will get much more attention than just a listing of names. It personalizes the contest and builds team spirit.

• Sales team stationery, including the team logo. Let OfficeMax, Staples, or Office Depot print up some team stationary, which you can use to announce major wins and events. Posting these accomplishments is a great idea. So is sending out a good-win announcement on sales team stationery, signed by sales management.

• Parking spot of the month for most new business. Put the name of the salesperson on the spot rather than *Employee of the Month*. It adds a personal touch when the salesperson drives up and sees *Bob Smith—Sales Leader*.

• The A club. Once a month, hold a sales strategy meeting attended only by the salespeople who are on pace for their year-to-date quota. You can make it really special by adding guest speakers, such as the vice president of marketing, the president, or a top technical person to speak on product knowledge.

The possibilities are endless. Be creative and start having fun. Make sure though that your salespeople are having fun too. Too many good ideas end up with the sales manager having the most fun and the salespeople "humoring" the boss.

Stay Focused or Pay Free Money

Many sales organizations give away free money. It happens when a salesperson receives cash or rewards for accomplishing a goal or task, but without a complete understanding of why she received the award. This usually occurs when sales organizations run too many contests, launch reward programs that last for months or even years, or when the people who initiated the event left the company a few years ago. Free money starts taking on a life of its own. The sales manager ends up paying out time, resources, and money for very little return.

Your primary responsibility is to stay focused on what the praise or reward is trying to accomplish. Having four contests running simultaneously can lead to a salesperson ending up with a reward but having difficulty tying a certain behavior to it. Does she take the money? You bet. But does she remember what she did to earn it? Now that is a different story. Keep the program focused and advertise it. Keep doing your S.O.S. and using your M²O/t's to keep them fresh and focused.

Praise and reward programs can be fun and exciting. They keep employee morale and motivation high. Most important, the interest level and enthusiasm you place on these efforts will have a direct correlation to the program's success. Everyone wins.

Chapter 9

Sales Meetings

Communication is a key part of any sales team's success. How often and how well a team communicates externally to its customers and internally to its members goes a long way to establishing a winning culture and long-term success. Internal communication generally occurs during sales meetings.

Sales meetings can be informal or formal, depending on the format and what needs to be discussed. They can be reactive: "OK, anyone have something else to add?" They can be Pro Active: "Today's agenda is in front of you and it should take no more than 30 minutes. Let's get started with Item 1." Sales meetings can take place over the phone, in person, or a mix of phone, video conferencing, and in person. They can take place online in a company chat room. The meeting's agenda can range from a simple "what happened last week" to a formal new product knowledge presentation.

A sales meeting can take on a life of its own. What are the secrets to successful sales meetings? How can you maximize the salesperson's time and the company's time so that out-of-the-field sales time and out-of-the-office management time are minimized? Let's look at some guidelines on how to have successful meetings.

When and How to Have
Successful Sales Meetings

Planning is the key. The success of a sales meeting is directly proportionate to the amount of time the sales manager puts into the planning of the meeting. From the once-a-week phone call to the once-a-year kickoff, the key to success is planning, which involves three areas:

- Agenda Planning
- Time Planning
- Content Planning

Before we review all three areas, we need to delineate between the weekly sales meeting and the all-sales team meeting. They have different goals. The weekly meeting is tactical. It covers current issues and can affect the sales team's tactics. The all-sales meeting, which takes place annually, semiannually, or quarterly, tends to be more strategic, cover more topics in depth, and can also include team-building activities. These meetings tend to cover the entire "Sales-Training Bicycle" in their scope and take anywhere from one to five days to achieve their objectives. How often the ProActive sales manager has weekly or all-sales meetings depends entirely on the situation. The sales manager should do an S.O.S. on the goals of these two meetings and determine the frequency of both. The agenda, the time duration, and the content of these meetings are all important.

Agenda Planning

The beginning is usually a good place to start, and the agenda—what needs to be covered in what sequence—is a good beginning. The agenda covers the pulse of the meeting, and therefore it has one rule: All sales meetings must have a written agenda. Whether in memo format, e-mail format, or written on the wipe board and reviewed before the meeting starts, a meeting with an agenda has a good chance of staying on track and being productive. Without a *written* agenda, attendees tend to wander off the path and productivity tends to diminish.

A well-thought-out agenda covers five areas.

1. *The Topics.* Weekly sales meetings should be brief and to the point. The agenda should be an interactive one and should

focus on tactical topics. The agenda should be strictly followed to keep the meeting focused and on schedule.

All-sales meetings should be organized around the five sales competencies: Selling Skills, Communication Skills, Presentation Skills, Product Knowledge, and Personal Growth. Some time can be spent on current topics as well, such as sales year-to-date and recent activities and successes. Keep the sales meeting moving by varying the topics and focusing on sales competencies. Make the topics interactive to encourage participation. Learning takes place when there is a transfer of ownership and participants are involved in the process.

Items that should be avoided in all-sales meetings include:

- *Long-Winded Success Stories.* In general, salespeople do not pick up good sales tips from hour-long sales success stories. What a waste of time. A good success story can be covered in less than 20 minutes.

- *Executive Speeches over 20 Minutes.* See above.

- *Long-Winded Competitive Assessments.* Usually they are of no real value, and usually they are wrong. Customers don't buy competitors; they buy solutions to needs. Subjective competitive assessments pump up the sales team but have little long-term value. If you must do a competitive assessment, stick with facts.

- *Any Speech After 4:00 P.M.* Sales meetings that last 12 or 16 hours defeat their own purpose. Limit the meetings to 6 to 8 hours a day, and schedule organized events in the evening. The sales team has nothing but work to talk about anyway, and having the sales team talk among themselves after the meeting leads to more learning than you can plan for during the day.

- *Corporate Human Resource or Internal Company-Finance Topics That Exceed 30 Minutes.* There are specific department issues that really should be covered. What we are talking about here are the overboard situations.

2. *The Time Allocated to Each Topic.* Each topic at the weekly sales meeting should be covered in 10 minutes or less. At the all-sales meeting, you should allocate up to 45 minutes per speech.

3. *Start and End Times.* It is important for the sales meeting to start and end on time. Stick to the agenda as closely as possible. Lock the late arrivals out of sessions if you must. Do not penalize the people who arrived on time by reviewing items some attendees may have missed by being late. If the late arrivals thought it was important, they would have been there on time.

4. *Flow of the Meeting.* Keep the flow of the meeting going. You should see yourself as a facilitator rather than a sales manager. Keep the discussions focused and to the point. Stop conversations that are going off to la-la land, and stop the "exception to the rule" discussions where the example the salesperson is using happens only once every 150 years.

5. *Logistics.* A meeting can live and die on its logistics. Is the room set up right? Is the phone connection hooked up and is the speakerphone working properly? Is the audiovisual equipment in working order? U-shaped, team, and conference-style seat setups are best for conversation. Theater style is best for presentations and follow-up question-and-answer sessions. Handouts and presentation material should be organized in a flow that mimics the sales meeting agenda. This may seem elementary, but too many sales meetings have lost momentum due to poor logistics.

Time Planning

The timing element for sales meetings is crucial and will vary according to the type of sales meeting.

* *Weekly Meetings.* When sales meetings are weekly, they should be held at the same time. The time should be scheduled during nonselling hours, which means before 8:30 A.M., after 4:30 P.M., or during lunch. Successful weekly sales meetings are focused, results-oriented, and generally 30 to 45 minutes long. They should be seen as tactical meetings and should stay focused on such topics as new information, weekly activity, new corporate information relative to the current sales activity, and updates on monthly or quarterly goals. Limit discussion or take

lengthy discussions off line to avoid wasting the time of the group.

Weekly web video meetings are becoming the norm. Why fly people in for a meeting when you can conference with them over the web? Your team will be much more productive having these web video meetings than spending four hours to fly in for a six-hour meeting. Invest in technology and be more ProActive.

- *All-Sales Meetings*. These meetings typically run two to three days, but may last as long as five. In these meetings it is important to vary the agenda. Make it exciting. Get the sales team involved in the meeting itself so that the learning experience is maximized and people have more fun. Let the team present in a team fashion. Have them work on sales skills or competitive information in a short results-oriented manner.

Meeting presenters should be limited to less than 45 minutes each. Meetings should start early, say at 7:30 or 8:00 A.M., and end near 4:00 or 4:30 P.M. After this time, most teams are "brain dead" and learning is at a minimum. After 5:00 P.M., team activities or role-play scenarios are the logical choice. Homework assignments for the next day, individually or in teams, are an effective way to make use of the evening hours. Schedule two or three 10- to 15-minute breaks. Allow an hour for lunch.

Start on time and stick to the agenda. Run on schedule. The ProActive sales manager has a well-prepared agenda and stays on schedule for content and timing.

Content Planning

The content of weekly meetings should be situational and focused on communication and tactical selling issues. Use weekly sales meetings to give short bursts of tactical information in a timely manner, and to provide an interactive communication vehicle. The "same place, same time, same topic, same seat" meetings may seem effective to some sales managers and some of the more vocal salespeople. However, they usually don't provide for two-way communication, which can only be planned for in the agenda. It all comes back down to a well-thought-out agenda.

The all-sales meetings should focus around the five sales competencies. The priority of topics should evolve around your S.O.S. What are the major informational issues needed to increase success? With your S.O.S. completed, you can begin to develop the agenda. There are many groups that will want in on the agenda as well because this is the only time to "meet with the entire sales team." If the topics meet your S.O.S., or if the topics are a company priority (remember, it is not *your* sales team; it belongs to the company), then fit them into the agenda, but try to keep them under 30 minutes. If you allocate the entire meeting into 30- to 45-minute segments, then finding an additional slot should be no problem.

Reactive and ProActive managers tend to organize content for all-sales meetings according to different priorities, as shown in the following comparison:

Reactive Manager	*ProActive Manager*
1. Product Knowledge	1. Selling Skills
2. Company Speakers	2. Communication/ Presentation Skills
3. Team Building	3. Product Knowledge
4. Free Time	4. Team Building
5. Communication Skills	5. Company Speakers

The agenda content should be adjusted based on your S.O.S. Typically, sales are made because salespeople can sell, not just because they have a wealth of product knowledge. Salespeople believe they need both product knowledge and sales skills. Combine the two and leverage the situation in role-plays or team-building exercises. As a manager, you can get product knowledge to your sales team in many different ways, including product literature, technical support, or Internet information. As a manager, you also know you lose most of your deals because you were outsold. Play the odds and focus your content around the skills or information you need to be successful.

Optional Meetings

Salespeople know value. They know whether something is important. If there are A players on the sales team, they will know what is important. If the sales meetings are important, the A salespeople will attend. C players will always attend anything that allows them to skip making sales calls, especially prospecting ones. The C players will always show up for sales meetings, either weekly or all-sales ones. The question is, How do you make sure the A salespeople find value to attend your sales meetings? Simply think about making some of the meetings optional.

Now it is at this point that sales managers say, "If I make some of the sales meetings optional, no one will come." This is exactly the point. If the sales meetings are a value-add, A players will always attend, because by definition, the meetings have a value. It's when the meetings start getting routine, boring, dull, and just plain mediocre that A players decide they can spend their time more productively.

Remember when near the end of your senior year in high school, things got a little loose and class content started slipping? You knew that there were certain classes you could skip and not fall too far behind. Then there were those classes that you couldn't miss without falling too far behind. You didn't cut those classes, right?

Such a class was Mr. Beyer's English class. Everyone knew that if you missed one day of his class, you got so far behind that it would take you days to catch up. Therefore, somehow, you always made it to class. Attendance was always high, the classes were participatory and high in value, and the pace was fast. Nice meetings, Mr. Beyer!

Just like your value-oriented high school classes, if a sales meeting has value, people will come. If the meetings are optional and have value, a few things happen. First, the manager is forced to keep the content high, relevant, and interactive. Second, the manager will keep to a tight agenda. A players have their time scheduled pretty tightly (which is why they are A players), and they will regard overlong meetings as a waste of time, regardless of content.

Finally, optional meetings put the responsibility for success on the salespeople. If they stop attending, cancel the meetings. It will only take a short while before the salespeople start complaining about the lack of communication within the sales team.

And all you have to do is claim innocence: "I had the meetings and no one came. Now you want the meetings? OK, I'll hold them, but only if you help make them a value-add. Deal?" This shift in responsibility is healthy for both the salesperson and the manager. It balances out the meetings from both perspectives and makes the meetings more valuable.

Make the sales meetings optional. When they are a high value-add, the sales team will knock your door down to come, and you will be perceived as a value-add sales manager. It will keep the agenda tight and the meeting participatory. It will allow both parties to share in the success. Great sales meetings do not happen because people show up every week. They are well thought out and are successful before the meeting even starts. It is another ProActive action a manager can take to stay one step ahead.

A rule of thumb about sales meetings: With a good agenda, they are usually 60 to 80 percent about future activity. They cover items on which you can take action. Without a proper agenda, you will spend numerous hours talking about history. And last time I checked, you can't change history.

Send these minutes out over e-mail. Set and send the agenda out for the next meeting a day ahead so people can prepare. If it's not on the agenda, it can't be discussed at the meeting. Pretty simple stuff.

Being prepared for meetings is tougher than it appears, but with the right planning and organization, you will have great, productive meetings that accomplish your team's goals.

Chapter 10

Create the ProActive Action Plan

Now it is time to put it all together. It is time for the sales management function in an organization to put into action what it wants and needs from the organization and to formalize its commitment to being ProActive.

It is time for a change.

As the sales manager, you need to create an action plan and communicate it to the organization and to your team. Formally communicate the organization's beliefs and goals.

The Coaching Wall of Principles

What do you believe in? What do you stand for? What are the bricks in your wall of principles? What bricks do you coach and counsel from? If you are a leader, you have bricks in your wall, and other people in your organization know exactly what to do without you having to tell them. If you are President Ronald Reagan, you have certain bricks in your wall. More defense, less government, evil empire, and so on. If you worked for President Reagan, and you had an idea for reducing the defense budget, knowing his wall, you would surmise your proposal would have little chance for success. President Reagan had bricks in his wall and communicated those bricks in almost every speech he gave.

What happens when you break a brick? Remember President George H.W. Bush and his brick, "Read my lips. No new taxes." When he broke that brick, it may have cost him the reelection.

Bricks are the foundation of an organization. They are the culture and the fiber. They are the reason why employees have pride in their job and enjoy working for their boss or their organization. They are the clear and consistent communication of the values and principles—up, down, and sideways in an organization.

So, what are the bricks in your coaching wall?

Dan Thompson of the Trane Corporation had his principles engraved on an actual brick and then gave one to everyone in his organization. His "coaching wall of principles" is shown in Figure 10-1.

Create your own brick wall. Get an 8 1/2 × 11-inch piece of paper and put four to six Post-it Notes on it. Go ahead; do it now. Then, on each Post-it Note, put down what you believe. This is the time for you to really think about what is important to you and to the organization. It's what you want to make sure everyone knows is important to you.

To put it another way, if you don't do this, how are you formally communicating to your employees, your boss, and your peers? How are they to know what's important? Do they have to guess? Create your brick wall now. To get you started, here are some potential bricks in your coaching wall.

Fun   Drive

Figure 10-1. The coaching wall of principles.

Coaching Wall of Principles		
Skill Improvement	Market Share	Profit
New Dealers	Fun	Make a Difference

Succeed	Make It Happen
Honesty	Employees First
Do It Now	Learn
Reward the Best	Only A Players
Invest in the People	Customer First
Grow 20 Percent/Year	Be Smart
Trust	Learn and Grow
Qualify	Market Share
Grow the Business	Always a Sale
Triumph	Listen
Own the Sales Cycle	Be ProActive

This is a short list, but when communicated formally, it takes on another meaning. Make sure your list is positive. Remember, leaders tell people what to do, not what not to do. "No more CC sales calls" should be stated as "Make five more AA sales calls per month." Put in the positive and ProActive action.

Now that you have your brick wall—your coaching wall—post it in your office. You need to communicate it formally to make sure everyone knows what you believe in. Guess what happens when your boss or your employees see this on your wall? Right. They start asking, "What is this?" And you will have a chance to communicate to all what your beliefs and goals are for the organization. These opportunities come along infrequently, so take advantage of them. Do it now.

You now may be asking yourself, "What good will filling out this brick wall and posting it in my office do? My employees already know these things are important to me." Want to bet? Go ask them and listen to the range of responses. You'll understand why great leaders post their code of conduct and state their beliefs right up front.

Remember the movie *Patton*? Remember the opening speech by George C. Scott? This was the communication of the bricks in his wall to all his troops, right up front. The scene was also put in the beginning of the movie to set the bricks for the audience as well.

Once you have your brick wall, update it on a quarterly or semiannual basis to keep it current and alive. Every CEO or president, including the President of the United States, makes an annual report—a restatement of the bricks he documented the year before. If the President of the United States has to create a brick wall, so should you. Watch what happens. Pretty soon, you will be viewed as someone who communicates goals to all employees in the organization.

Remember that in Chapter 1 we said this is what leaders do. They communicate their goals and ideas in a formal way. Leaders communicate what is important and do not leave room for guessing. Leaders have brick walls. Put yours up for all to see. Formally state to all what is important. What do you want your employees and boss to do, assuming they know what is important to you and to the sales team? The coaching wall is a formal communication device and a ProActive tool for the sales manager.

Setting Goals and Making Them Work

You have heard it many times before. If you do not have any written goals, how will you know if you have accomplished what you set out to do? The answer to this question usually consists of an excuse:

> "I just don't have the time to write goals."

> "I haven't yet gotten around to writing goals."

> "The problem is I write them down and then never take any action on them."

Join the crowd. Only about 20 percent of the managers we meet have written goals. Even fewer have consistently implemented goals or measure themselves against their own goals. Yet, these are the very goals the managers claim are important to them! We could spend chapters on why people have a hard time following their goals, but let's focus on how we can implement goals that work.

There are three key points about goals you need to focus on. Make sure that:

1. You write down and update your short- and long-term goals.
2. Your goals are measurable.
3. You communicate your goals.

Short-Term vs. Long-Term Goals

In the movie *What about Bob?* the actor Bill Murray plays a de-pressed patient under psychiatric care. His doctor, played by Richard Dreyfuss, advises him to get better by taking "little baby steps." During the movie Bill Murray constantly repeats "little baby steps, little baby steps." This is how we need to treat goals, like little baby steps.

What are your short-term and long-term goals? If you begin with the short term, you then can focus on the long term. Step one: What are the top five goals—either work-related or per-sonal—that you want to accomplish over the next 90 days? Write them down. Now. *Please.* Now! It's important (Figure 10-2).

Now take this book to a copier and make a copy of the page containing your goals. Then post it where you will see it every day. We are trying to get you to focus on the goals you want for yourself. Post the page in a visible spot, on the refrigerator, on the bathroom mirror, or in your office—anywhere you'll have to look at it frequently.

Please do not put it in a drawer. If you see your goals fre-quently over the next few days, you will increase your chances of actually doing them. If you post them and review them daily, you will focus on them. Constantly update and balance them. It is important to have a balance between the short-term/tactical and the long-term/strategic goals. Review your two sets of goals and make sure they are in synch with each other.

One other thing about goals: They must be measurable.

Measurable Goals

Now go back and review these goals to make sure they are mea-surable. If you can't measure something, why do it? Does this

Figure 10-2. The ProActive manager's goals.

Top 5 Goals—3 Months

1. _____

2. _____

3. _____

4. _____

5. _____

Top 5 Goals—12 Months

1. _____

2. _____

3. _____

4. _____

5. _____

sound familiar? Goals need to have a measurable quality about them. Consider the following goals:

> "I will buy a new car by October 1."
>
> "I will get my resume together by next Friday and use two PowerHours next week to do it."
>
> "I will take the family on a Saturday vacation this month."

These are measurable, short-term goals. When you write them down, it is amazing what action you will take to accomplish them. I had a short-term goal to finish my company's business plan by the end of the month. It is the 30th of the month. I am going to finish the business plan and I have allocated time this morning and later today to do just that. I will get it done. It's a measurable goal I have written down and I will see my goal written down on this Post-it Note all day. Oh, and one more thing—I have communicated this goal to a lot of people, and I want to show them I can achieve goals I set for myself.

Communication

You need to communicate your goals to your boss, your employees, your friends, and your family.

Communication will help you stay focused; it will allow other people to assist you reach your goals. For example, when you have communicated your goals, other people can assist you by offering advice, subject matter knowledge, or relevant experiences. With other people helping you, you will reach more goals than you thought possible.

Do any of these quotes sound like you?

> "I can't post my goals. People will laugh at me. I'll feel silly."

> "I know what my goals are. Why do I need anyone else's help?"

> "I am afraid to write down my goals since I may not make all of them and I'll feel like a failure."

Very few people make all their goals. In fact, if you do make all of your goals all the time, you may need to stretch yourself more. Most of the time, you may come up a little short on the really tough ones.

You also need to look at the progress you made toward the goals and be somewhat satisfied at that progress. Refine the goals and start again. "The journey is the reward," according to former Apple Computer CEO John Sculley in his book by the same title. And it is true. Take a small step toward each goal and enjoy the journey. Focus on the goals, and communicate them so you have created a support structure. If some of your employees came to you right now and told you their top goals for the next 90 days, and asked if you could help them achieve these goals, what would you do? Even money says you would make a special effort to help them. It goes both ways.

Write your goals down. Make sure they are measurable. Communicate them. Only then will you be able to measure your progress and feel like you are getting somewhere.

What if you went on a vacation without a goal? "We're going on vacation."

"Where?"

"I don't know, but I'll know when we get there."

State your goals the way you would state your vacation plans: "The first two weeks in August, we are going to Washington to see the White House, the Jefferson Memorial, and the Washington Monument."

Or in sales management terms: "By the end of the first quarter, the sales team will call on 50 AA accounts, receive two days of sales training, have one day of new product training, and will accomplish its stated revenue goals."

Which vacation would you rather go on? Which journey are you on today? Write down your goals, make sure they are measurable, and communicate them. Your goals will come alive, get you focused, and end up working for you.

Go and Make a Difference

Being a ProActive sales manager means having the tools necessary to be one step ahead. It's all about applying the tools you need to be ProActive.

I hope that you have enjoyed reading this book and will be able to apply many of the tools that have been discussed. I need to let you in on a little secret, however. Ready? It's shocking, but true: Less than 35 percent of the people attending ProActive sales management classes actually use these tools!

A few years ago, I asked why. Why would managers leave a training session saying these ideas are the greatest thing since sliced bread, and then not implement them? We investigated and found that there seemed to be three consistent answers: the A-B-C bell curve for managers, lack of the right support structure, and lack of self-discipline.

The A-B-C Bell Curve Applies to Managers as Well

It's disheartening but true: The bell curve applies to managers. That means there are A managers, B managers, and C managers. If we follow the rules in this book, and focus on the As only, then there is a happy ending. Like you, I may feel the need to help the Bs and Cs, but I follow the rule of teaching to the As. Given the 30 to 35 percent "stick factor" of the tools in the management sessions, these results seem better than one could hope for. But, being the eternal optimist, I always hope to influence the Bs and Cs as well.

The difference between A sales managers and B and C sales managers is small. All B and C sales managers have to do is S.O.S., develop some M²O/t's, pick three or four tools, and use them consistently. The A managers have been taking notes while reading this book and have already started to implement some of the tools. The Bs are thinking about it, and the Cs . . . well, come on, get with the program! The Miller 17 is easy to implement. So is the Profile of a Successful Performer. Get going.

The Support Structure Back at the Office

If you have a great work environment in which to learn and grow, the tools described in this book should provide you with a communication platform from which to create a mutual support structure back at the office. Don't just focus on revenue. Review the 30-60-90, the Miller 17, the concept of Frequency and Competency, and the formula $R = F \times C$. A wise person once told me that people learn best when they teach someone else. So the more you preach the tools you are going to put into place, the more you are going to learn and master them.

Communication is the key to successfully implementing these ProActive sales management tools within an organization that already has good support. Have a meeting with your boss, your peers, and your subordinates. Present your new goals to them, show them the tools, and ask for their input and support. Formally work to keep changing the culture of the organization. And remember, the memory of these tools will fade in a matter of weeks. Do it now. Implement the tools you want to use.

S.O.S. your situation. During your next few PowerHours, come up with a strategy to accomplish your M²O/t's.

We get lots of requests from sales managers who have been exposed to ProActive sales management tools, asking whether it is OK to use techniques such as R = F × C and M²O/t for internal sales presentations and presentations to their senior management. You bet. Use them and take ownership of them. Don't call it a Miller 17. Personalize it. Once you have taken ownership of the tools, they are *your* tools, and you have increased the likelihood of implementing them. The key is communication, both formal and informal.

If your boss has not read this book or been exposed to its philosophies, or if you have a less than optimal support environment, you need to do the same thing. Communicate your beliefs and implement your tools as soon as possible. You may run into others who will embrace your new tools with less enthusiasm than you. That's a polite way of saying they are going to look at you like you are an alien and will treat you with the same amount of disrespect they always have.

But remember: *This too shall pass.* The A-B-C curve applies to bosses too. Wait for your time to shine. And in the meantime . . .

Implement anyway: How much more trouble can you be in? These processes work, and they are probably better than what you are doing now. Take a risk and go for it, and communicate what you are doing. They pay you to make decisions, so make a few.

Or . . .

Change the situation. This is different from giving up. Go find a situation where your skills can be used more than they are today. The clock is ticking, and staying in a position where you are not effective is a losing proposition. Use your PowerHours to update your resume, make some new contacts, and start networking. It's your career, and BMWC (bitching, moaning, whining, complaining) usually has little positive impact. Changing the situation is the answer, and you want to change it on your terms.

Your support structure is important. It is very hard, if not impossible, to run a sales organization without one. With good support in place, your odds of creating change and implementing some ProActive tools are high. Get your team together and ask for help and support. You may be surprised to find how many team members you actually have.

Chapter 11

The Technology of Sales

The goal of every sales manager is to create leverage. Without leverage, a 1:1 ROI is all that is available, and that is not acceptable. Quotas go up faster than headcount and resources, so increasing leverage is the only way to stay ahead. To stay ahead, sales management must lead in the adaption of technology change.

Sales Force Automation (SFA) and Customer Resource Management (CRM) systems—hosted or as Software as a Service (SaaS) models—offer quite a bit for the sales team. However, these systems do a great job at tracking results, and not activities. Tracking the things that cause revenue to happen should be the goal of every sales manager, and technology should be used in three vital areas:

- Decreasing Order Time
- Increasing the Salesperson's Ability to Sell
- Increasing Breadth and Depth

Decreasing Order Time

Sales cycle time, or the time it takes for a customer to place an order, has gotten out of control. Too many sales organizations have charted their sales process without tracking how their customers buy. Using automation to leverage this opportunity is a must.

Identifying a buy process in the buyer's organization and

then tracking the activities is key to technology productivity. Otherwise, too much is left to chance. Working a process with the prospect is in the best interest of both parties. Many tools are available to help sales organizations do this. Using visual flow charts such as the Trip-Tik in ProActive Selling™ (see Figure 11-1), creating account plans with mapping software such as Mind-Jet™ (see Figure 11-2), and having web collaboration meetings using WebEx™ instead of only face-to-face calls are just a few of the ways sales organizations are getting higher productivity gains and a decrease in the average selling time.

The trend is clear: Salespeople do not want to travel as much as they have been, sales managers and CFOs do not want to pay for that travel, and customers are getting tired of 60-minute meetings when a web event can cover everything in 20 minutes. This trend is now too mainstream to ignore any longer.

Tools like these give you leverage with prospects and customers. Have some of your A players experiment with them so you can figure out what to implement. And the sooner the better!

Increasing the Salesperson's Ability to Sell

It's all about the ability to satisfy the customer. But sales calls are just one sales activity. The ability to accomplish more and more activities using technology is increasing sales productivity.

- Joint Contract Negotiations
- Worldwide Sales Contracts with All Parties Online and with Full Video
- Prospecting by Sending People to a Live Web Session
- Getting Online Referrals
- User Demos When the Prospect Chooses What Time to Attend
- On-Demand Sales Call Support with Web and Video Chat

There are many ways that technology can lower costs and increase productivity. When I travel for business, especially in Europe and Asia, I have video VoIP chat sessions with my office

(*text continues on page 232*)

Figure 11-1. Trip-Tik—How Customers Want to Buy.

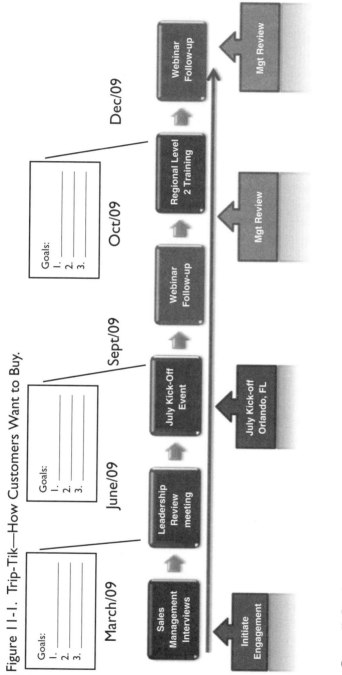

Overall Goals:

Figure 11-2. MindJet™ Account Plan example.

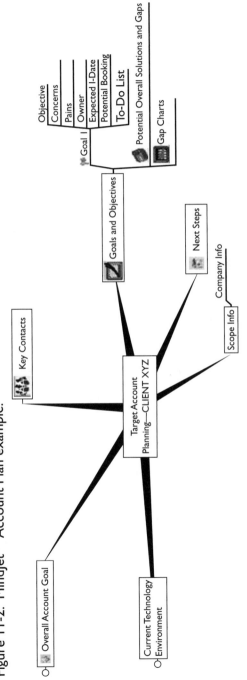

(and even with my kids). If my 13-year-old twins can use video and chat technology to be more productive—they do not want to take the time to write me an e-mail . . . how "yesterday"— then so can you.

Increasing Breadth and Depth

Why is it that sales managers are screaming for increased breadth and depth in their major accounts, but will not turn to technology for help in increasing revenues?

- A company that sells to architects uses video references to gain more appeal inside a firm. It schedules an hour for the firm to log on and see an application from one of its current partners.
- A research company gives various departments web access to information that the marketing department is using, thereby encouraging intracompany communications.
- Customers of an office supply company track company holidays, personal vacations, and company anniversaries for its clients allowing it access to all departments within a company.
- A large multinational company has a monthly 30-minute video webcast update for all employees worldwide, keeping them abreast of the most recent purchases and uses of its products and services. The company's worldwide head of purchasing is host of the update.

What are you waiting for?

The New Process

Technology now requires you to stand your sales process on its head. No more adding technology piecemeal to the old sales process. Now is the time for a technology-centric sales process that may require some individual interaction, either on the phone or in person. Measure the sales process in technology terms, then add in the customer, and *then* add your sales process. This is a different way to think. It is highly web-centric, rather than selling-centric.

The key is to think of a two-way sales process that requires your prospect to use technology to buy. For example, you can offer a 5 percent discount to customers who use online-only contracts, proposals, and meetings. This will ensure a faster sales cycle and a better close rate. You'll find it's worth the five points you are giving up.

"I'll get you that proposal by Friday" is a thing of the past. Today's it's, "Let's get on a web event and go over the proposal and contract. We can do that online tomorrow at 10:00 a.m. We can have your purchasing manager on as well. We'll get final approval and ship the same day."

Makes you think.

The New Dashboard

Do you track the number of calls at a VP level? Number of web events? How long a sale has been in a certain sales stage? Average sale length? Average talk time per day for an inside sales team? Number of customer touches? ProActive success metrics to show shape and velocity of a buy/sales process?

Do you know what training each of your sales and sales support team have had, and what they need? How are you aligning your sales team's needs with the application of technology? Do you even know how many words per minute your sales team types?

Dashboards are now more ProActive and more metric-centric. No, this is not micromanaging. It's managing the activities that cause success. It's keeping the team on track. When you are going down the road at 6 mph or at 60 mph, how many times do you look at the road and at your dashboard? Now imagine 200 mph. That's where we are today. You gather quarterly information? You are kidding, right?

Getting Things Done in a Team Sell

Technology has now created the ability to team sell in a cost-effective manner. Team sell used to mean four- or six-leg sales calls, along with the cost of flying everyone to the customer site, or to the home office. Not anymore. Team sell now means that both the client and the sales team meet virtually. They save time and effort doing so, not to mention gain an edge over the competition. What can you do to encourage 20 percent of your top accounts to participate in a team sell environment?

Getting Things Done with Your Customers

Your customers are looking for leadership when it comes to buying things less expensively with less time and less risk. It seems the smaller the company, the more advanced they are at using technology on a daily basis with their customers. Send your top 20 customers webcams and have a video review every month, rather than the conference call that everyone mutes and no one really pays attention to (see Figure 11-3). The game changes when you get everyone on video.

An example is of video, text, and chat all in one meeting with multiple users from WebEx, a Cisco company.

Change starts small and from the bottom up. What can you do right now in a ProActive way to encourage your sales team to use technology with your prospects and customers, rather than internal tracking and sales spying? The choice is yours. The name of the game is sales and margins. Sales management needs to pay attention to both.

Technology is forcing management to pay attention to the bottom line as well as the top line. The old game of hiring more salespeople is all but through. So, be ProActive. Gain leverage. And watch your sales take off.

Discipline and the Will to Change

Self-discipline is the will to make things happen. Anyone can do something once or twice, but the true measure of a superstar is

Figure 11-3. A web-collaboration sales call.

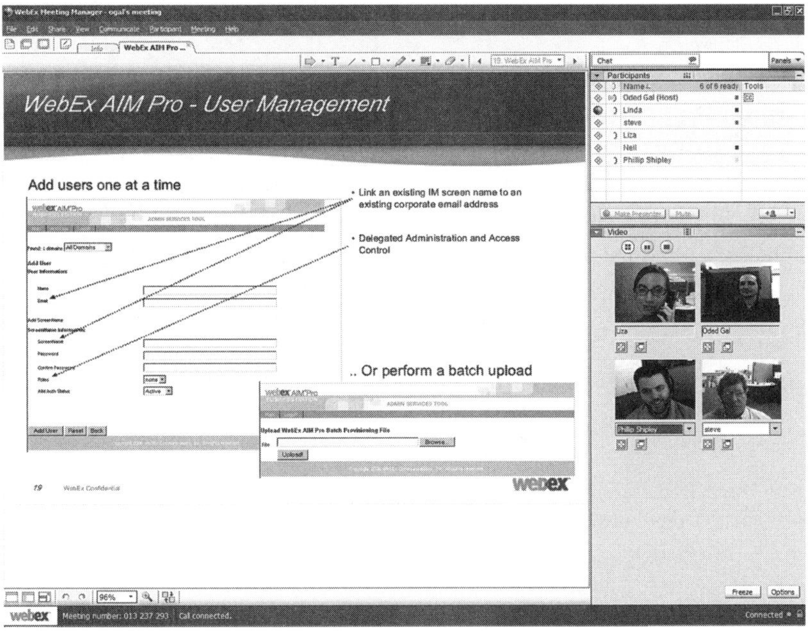

An example of video, text, and chat all in one meeting with multiple users from WebEX, a Cisco company.

the ability to perform a task well again and again. It takes will-power and discipline to get into shape, to be responsible, and to do the right things. It takes willpower and discipline to imple-ment change, to face fears, and to do something others "know" you will fail at.

The importance of change is illustrated by the following quotes:

"If you are not changing faster than the environment, then the end is definitely in sight."

"Without change, imagine where we would be."

"Change is the tool of all master craftsmen."

"Change, in the right hands, makes the best even better."

You have the technological, the strategic, and the tactical tools you need. You have the processes. You have the time during your PowerHours to strategize and implement the activities and ideas that will make you more effective than ever.

Change.

Change yourself and your sales culture. Be an agent of change. We learn more from our losses than our victories, so go change things up. If you get 80 percent right, go ahead and figure out the other 20 percent. Get 80 percent of *that* right and you are at 96 percent. Not bad. It's what leaders do all the time. It's what you will be doing, beginning tomorrow.

Index